ANCIENT SEMITIC CIVILIZATIONS

Ancient

Semitic Civilizations

SABATINO MOSCATI

Professor of Semitic Philology
in the University of Rome

CAPRICORN BOOKS

G. P. Putnam's Sons   *New York*

This work was originally published in Italy
by Gius Laterza & Figli of Bari, under the
title *Storia e Civilta dei Semiti.*

MANUFACTURED IN THE UNITED STATES OF AMERICA

ACKNOWLEDGEMENTS

The author wishes to express his gratitude to the following scholars for help in obtaining permission to reproduce photographs, and to the following institutions for granting permission: Mr. R. D. Barnett and the British Museum; Prof. H. Cazelles and the Louvre; His Excellency Dr. Naji al Asil and the Directorate General of Antiquities, Baghdad; Dr. N. Avigad and the Hebrew University, Jerusalem; Prof. A. Jamme and the American Foundation for the Study of Man; the Dumbarton Oaks Collection; Prof. C. Giannelli and the Vatican Library; Dr. A. Caquot and the Archaeological Department, Addis Ababa.

CONTENTS

CONTENTS

ILLUSTRATIONS
Following page 128.

ILLUSTRATIONS IN THE TEXT

MAPS

FOREWORD

The story of this book begins ten years ago. While teaching Semitic archaeology in the University of Rome, I found myself faced by the fact that whereas there were various general works on Semitic languages taken as a group, there was no such work about the peoples who spoke those languages.

Yet these peoples are united by many bonds of social conditions, religious conceptions, and artistic forms. It seemed to follow that a book setting forth the essential outline of their forms of civilization and of their distinctive common traits not only could but should be written.

The book appeared in Italian in 1949; a German edition followed in 1953, a French one in 1955, and another German one in the same year. An English edition was still lacking; and it is with especial pleasure that I now offer it to the public of Great Britain and of America, to whom I am bound by so many cherished memories. May my colleagues who invited me to lecture in those countries, and the students who followed my lectures with such intelligent interest, and all the friends who showed me such kindness, each see in this book a token of my grateful remembrance of them.

I must also crave their indulgence. In a brief synopsis such as this, no more can be given than a sketch of the salient features of the ancient Semitic civilizations. There would have been no point in loading the text with names and numbers; better to restrict oneself to the outstanding elements, to the more characteristic aspects of the life and thought of the peoples described.

There was also the question of chronological limits. I have here restricted myself to the ancient, or what may be called "classical" period of Semitic civilizations. This gives us the whole of the historical existence of the Babylonians and Assyrians and of the Canaanites; but the treatment of the Hebrews is broken off with the loss of their political independence; that of the Aramaeans and that of the Arabs with Hellenism and Islam respectively, for both of these phenomena take us beyond the limits of national and Semitic history; that of the Ethiopians, when the Islamic conquest of the regions to the east and to the north of them shut them up in a local, African setting. This is admittedly an imperfect delimitation; but would not any other have been equally or more so? Moreover, only this ancient phase seems to me to exhibit those common traits, linking together all the Semitic peoples, of which I have spoken above. When civilizations pass beyond the limits of their own environment to become assimilated into wider cultural circles, they thereby pass outside the scope of such a work as this.

A final word: with each new edition I have revised the book in the light of the continual advance of archaeological discovery and of scholarship in general, and in that of the opinions expressed by reviewers, and of my own. Each edition, therefore, and this is especially true of the present English one, has aimed at being not a translation, but a new work.

Sabatino Moscati.

Rome, March 31st, 1957.

CHAPTER ONE

THE STAGE

THE vast Asiatic continent opens out at its western extremity into a broad peninsula, bounded on three sides by the sea, and linked by a land-bridge with Africa. This peninsula is called Arabia: a great desert or half-desert expanse, giving place in the north to a mountain-strip fronting the eastern Mediterranean, called Palestine in the south and Syria in the north. In the northeast the natural frontier is formed by the great curve of the mountains of Armenia and Iran; but here we are beyond the reach of the desert, for between the two great rivers Tigris and Euphrates, between the desert and the mountains, lies yet another region, and a singularly fertile one, called Mesopotamia, that is, the land between the rivers.

These three regions taken together—Arabia, Syria-Palestine, and Mesopotamia—form a geographical unity, which was in its day the stage of an important act in the drama of humanity. The peoples who were the actors in these dramatic episodes played the parts inevitably assigned to them by their natural conditions. On the one hand, the distinctions imposed by geographical factors brought about the emergence of peoples historically and politically individualized; on the other hand, the fundamental geographical unity bound them into an interdependence, thanks to which impulses originating in one sector had repercussions upon all the others.

The whole coastline of the Arabian peninsula is marked by its mountains, which rear themselves up, never far from the sea, to descend towards the interior upon a plateau sloping gently down

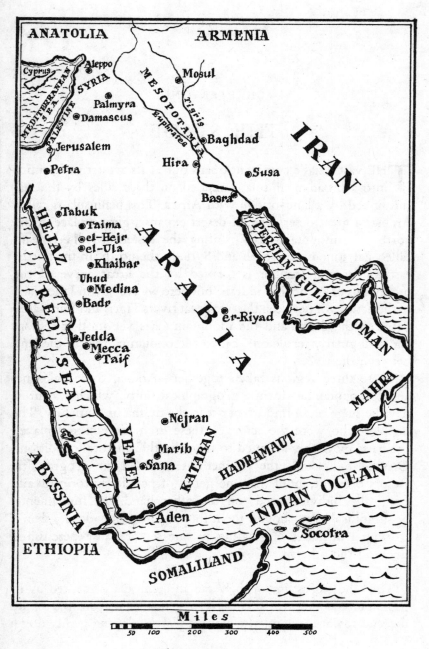

ANATOLIA   ARMENIA

Cyprus

Aleppo

MEDITERRANEAN SEA

SYRIA

MESOPOTAMIA

Mosul

Tigris

Euphrates

Palmyra

Damascus

PALESTINE

Jerusalem

Baghdad

IRAN

Petra

Hira

Susa

Basra

Tabuk

Taima

el-Hejr

el-Ula

Khaibar

Uhud

Medina

Badr

ARABIA

er-Riyad

PERSIAN GULF

HEJAZ

RED SEA

Jedda

Mecca

Taif

OMAN

MAHRA

Nejran

Marib

YEMEN

Sana

KATABAN

HADRAMAUT

INDIAN OCEAN

ABYSSINIA

Aden

Socotra

ETHIOPIA

SOMALILAND

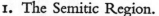

Miles

50   100   200   300   400   500

1. The Semitic Region.

towards Mesopotamia and the Persian Gulf. The outskirts of this plateau bear sparse and stunted vegetation; its interior is occupied by the vast barren sand-wastes of the Arabian desert.

The rivers that run down from the mountains are of no great size. Some of them are swallowed up into the ground, to reappear a considerable distance away in the midst of the arid sands. Round these oases is centred the wandering life of the tribes of the inner desert, for whom water is indeed the "best of things", the most precious and desirable of the elements. The oases are the saving gift of nature amid the parched wastes that have fallen to the lot of the people of Arabia. It happens, however, that the population centred around them becomes too numerous for their modest resources of fertility, and the tribes are forced to range farther afield in restless search for new bases.

Nearer the coast a more settled way of life is possible. The Hejaz, over against Egypt, has some little harbours, and its fertile oases have from the remotest times been peopled by settled groups, living chiefly by the trade which passes through them on the road to the north, through Mecca and Medina to Palestine and Syria.

Further to the south lies the Yemen, part of which faces the Ethiopian coast of Africa, while the rest faces the Indian Ocean. This is the most fertile region of the whole Arabian peninsula. The richness and variety of its products, and the mildness of its climate, in vivid contrast to the baking hinterland, won for it in ancient times its name of "Arabia Felix", that is, Arabia the Fortunate. These conditions inevitably determined, from the first millennium before Christ, the establishment in this region of stable political organizations, whose influence extended to the Ethiopian coast opposite in the form of a vast commercial system and of movements of colonization.

Taken as a whole, however, Arabia is the least rich of the regions we are now describing. Its vast expanse of desert rock and sand, broken only here and there by patches of vegetation, and the lack, in all its great stretch of coastline, of natural harbours of any size, imposed upon it an extreme isolation, thanks to which its position between Asia and Africa did not avail to make of it a commercial highway or the place of passage of migrating peoples. The coming and going of traders and of armies was confined to the Mediterranean region to the north of Arabia, while the desert remained aloof and unaffected by all the turmoil of history, preserving almost without change the characteristic features of its inhabitants and of their way of life. The powerful states which ruled in the north (Babylonia and Assyria, Byzantium and Persia) for long shut off the desert nomads from the fertile lands which they coveted. Only the decline of Byzantine power and the collapse of Persia, in the seventh century of the Christian era, allowed the Arabs, united by Islam, to burst forth from their desert in that great flood which was to sweep impetuously so far as central Asia and so far as France.

Very different in its natural features and consequently in its historical lot was the long narrow mountain border of the desert along the Mediterranean coast. While Arabia was poor in roads and harbours, Syria and Palestine, marked out by nature as an important zone of communication, were to see the constant passage of many peoples and of many forms of culture. In ancient times this region, set between the mighty political and economic powers of Mesopotamia and Egypt, was the inevitable outlet and testing-ground of their military and commercial ambition. In the middle ages it was overrun by the Moslem armies moving against Byzantium. In our own days it has remained the object of the great powers' effort to secure control of the means of communication between Europe and Africa in the West, and the Middle and Far East.

This region presents the general appearance of rows of mountains rising in tiers parallel with the sea. Along the whole length of this mountain mass, however, there runs a deep and clearcut depression, following approximately the course of two rivers, the Orontes in the north and the Jordan in the south. The Orontes, rising in Upper Syria, runs between two mountain walls that rise to as high as 10,000 feet: the range nearer to the sea is called Lebanon, and that nearer to the desert, Antilebanon.

The Lebanon range possesses vast forests of pine, cypress and cedar, a fact of the utmost commercial importance, since both Mesopotamia and Egypt are almost entirely destitute of building timber. The coast has good natural harbours, where there arose flourishing ports. This region was the home of the Phoenicians, the great merchant and mariner people of ancient times, whose skill and hardihood and colonizing zeal brought them to all the coasts of the Mediterranean, and beyond into the Atlantic, and to the tin-mines of Britain.

Eastwards from the Orontes, Antilebanon runs down to a region dotted with oases, around which grew up important cities. One of the most celebrated of these was Palmyra, the centre of a small independent state, and a stage-point of the important route joining Syria with Mesopotamia. Further to the south lies the oasis of Damascus, with its flower-gardens, watered by the rivers that flow down from the mountains. These cities were as a rule prevented from forming great political forces by their position between powers much more mighty than they; hence they tended rather to remain little independent states, of commercial rather than political importance. The same is true also of the cities of the Phoenician coast, whose more or less thinly veiled subjection to the suzerainty of the great powers did not in the least hinder them from attaining their supremacy in commerce by sea.

Phoenicia extends south beyond the Lebanon range, as far as the boundary of Palestine proper. Here too the mountain bulk is split by a river: the Jordan, famous above all, like the whole of this region, for its place in sacred history. Twice in its course this river broadens out into lakes: the little Lake of Tiberias in the north, and the Dead Sea in the south. Between the Lake of Tiberias and the Mediterranean lies Galilee, with Samaria to the south of it; and yet further south Judaea, with its thrice-holy city of Jerusalem.

Jerusalem lies at an altitude of about 2,600 feet. The surrounding region does not rise to much greater heights than this, and descends towards the sea to a sandy beach with few harbours. The terrain becomes more and more sandy as one goes southwards towards the Sinaitic peninsula, which is the limit of Palestine and of the continent of Asia. Sinai forms a bridge leading into Africa, into the rich valley of Egypt; but this journey is a difficult one, and travellers often preferred to brave the hazards of the sea, and embark for Egypt in the Phoenician ports.

Palestine and Syria may be called fertile lands, and have been cultivated from very remote times, in a continual process whereby pastoral peoples, coming from the desert, adopted by stages a settled and agricultural way of life. These infiltrations were not always peaceful ones, and violent inroads from the desert, along with those of the armies of the neighbouring powers, subjected this region to a series of devastating episodes, in accordance with that destiny which seems to have been the historical heritage of the best-known of its peoples, the Hebrews.

Herodotus called Egypt a gift of the Nile; a similar expression might be used of Mesopotamia, for its rivers are its life.

The Tigris and the Euphrates have nowadays a common mouth; in ancient times this was not so, and they ran parallel with each other to flow separately into the sea, which at that time extended much further north than now. The silt continually deposited as the current which bore it slowed down in the estuary brought about in the course of centuries the continual recession of the sea and the formation of the delta in which the two rivers came to unite their waters. Hence the ancient cities which had arisen on the coast came to lie further and further from the sea to which they owed their prosperity, and their ruins were engulfed by the sands of the desert.

These two great rivers take their rise amid the eternal snows of the Armenian mountains, which rise in places to altitudes of over 13,000 feet. From these heights they hurl themselves upon the plain, and here, where sand succeeds to rock, their impetuous course is checked, and its force tends to find an outlet in floods and in changes of course. These phenomena reach their culminating point in spring and summer, when the increase in the volume of water gives rise to sudden and capricious inundations, to the great detriment of the cultivated land. Man soon turned his hand, however, to the task of taming the wild element, and converting it into a source of prosperity; in very remote times he undertook the construction of a network of canals designed to receive the floodwaters and distribute them systematically. The whole of Mesopotamia's ancient literature is permeated by the memory of this great work, and at all periods Mesopotamian sovereigns regarded the maintenance of the canal system as one of their greatest titles to honour.

Beyond the region served by the canals lies that of the everlasting swamp, a treacherous plain of shallow waters overgrown with huge reeds, with here and there islets of more solid ground. Assyrian artists have given us pictures of refugees fleeing before the invader into the marshlands on little rafts, or hiding in the maze of reeds.

The extreme differences in the terrain traversed by the rivers, from eternal snows to torrid sands, correspond to differences in the Mesopotamian climate. Assyria in the north is in certain zones extremely cold, whereas Babylonia in the south swelters from May to November under an extreme of heat rendered more intolerable by the high degree of humidity; here the sun is naturally regarded as an agent of death and destruction, a torturer of man and beast.

The mountains in the north are rich in minerals: gold, silver, lead, iron and copper are to be found there in remarkable abundance; contracts have come down to us for the acquisition of metals brought by caravans from the north. The Mesopotamian subsoil is rich in other natural resources, such as naphtha and bitumen; the latter was widely used in ancient times by the Assyrian boatbuilders. Finally, the soil of this region is peculiarly suited to the raising of cereals.

From the mountains there descend also upon Mesopotamia the communication routes from the north and from the east. The history of this region is therefore in great part the history of the struggles for control over these routes, and so over the valley to which they gave access. It was to the mountains that Mesopotamian kings had constantly to direct their attention and their expeditions; and from the mountains came those who destroyed the Mesopotamian powers.

Nature made Syria and Palestine the inevitable meeting-place and battleground of all the movements, commercial, military and migratory, of the Near East. Geographically this narrow strip of land was the junction between three continents: the desert forced land communication between Asia and Africa into a great arc skirting the northern edge of the Arabian sands, while the road to Eastern Europe branched off in Upper Syria, thence to cross the Taurus into Asia Minor, making for Constantinople. As for the sea-routes, the importance of the Phoenician ports needs no explanation save the remark that it was enhanced by the difficulties opposed by mountain or desert to land communications around the Mediterranean.

In particular, from ancient times the most convenient and frequented passage from Syria to Egypt was by the sea-route. The advantages offered by the Phoenician ports were too great for many merchants and travellers to risk the dangers of the Sinaitic desert, which breaks the land route into Africa, although there was a route across that desert, leading from the southern Palestinian plain to the delta of the Nile. Palestine was poor in ports, and hence the bulk of maritime commerce tended to pass through the Phoenician ports.

The road from Syria to Mesopotamia is not a long one; by going up to Aleppo, the traveller leaves only a short tract of desert to be crossed before reaching the Euphrates. From that point on he may follow that river, or cross it and follow its northern tributaries towards the Tigris. To the south of this artery of trade there was a more modest caravan-route which from Damascus made straight for the middle Euphrates, cutting across the desert, and passing through the fertile oasis of Palmyra.

Communications with Arabia were more difficult. On the whole, the least inconvenient method was to go by the Red Sea to the coast, and thence penetrate into the interior; but the commercial communities of the Hejaz, and further to the south the prosperous states of Arabia Felix, knew also from the earliest times another trade-route, leading, roughly parallel with the coast, through Medina and Mecca, and then following the line of the oases into Southern Palestine, whence it continues into Syria. Some caravan-routes of much smaller importance cross the whole breadth of the peninsula, descending the gentle slope of the plateau to the Persian Gulf and to Mesopotamia.

Upper Syria is all but cut off from Asia Minor, and consequently from Europe, by the barrier of the mountains, but there is one road which crosses them directly and links up with the road to the north. This is the road through which the Arabs in the middle ages repeatedly tried to penetrate to the heart of the Byzantine Empire.

Both the history and the civilization of the peoples who lived in all these regions were shaped by the natural conditions of their environment. The various movements of migration or of conquest were influenced by the economic and climatic factors that rule the lives of men; their direction was determined by the natural lines of communication, and the possession of the latter, with the hold it gave over the whole life of the region, determined the course of history. States were born and grew up in a geographical background which allotted them here an enduring unity, there a perpetual state of division. The forms assumed by their civilization reflected their environment, and drew from it their strengths and their weaknesses.

At the same time, the balance of peoples, of states, and of cultural forms existing at any given moment within the area was always subject to influences from without. Dwelling at the meeting-point of the three great continents of the ancient world, Asia, Africa and Europe, the inhabitants of these lands could not fail to assimilate, to fuse together, and to transmit the cultural elements which all those continents contributed.

CHAPTER TWO

THE PLAYERS

IN the area described in the preceding chapter there dwelt, from the beginnings of history and who knows how long before that, peoples remarkably alike in their characteristics—the peoples whom we call Semitic.

This name is derived from a passage in the Bible: the tenth chapter of the book of Genesis, where we have an account of the relationships between the various peoples known to the writer, in the form of a genealogy of their descent from the sons of Noah. In this genealogical table the list of the sons of Shem includes Aram, Ashur and Eber, that is to say, the Aramaeans, the Assyrians and the Hebrews. The term "Semitic" was therefore adopted by European scholars towards the end of the eighteenth century as a common designation for that group of peoples to which the Aramaeans, Assyrians and Hebrews belong, a group whose interrelation is immediately evident in their languages. The use of the term was subsequently extended and modified with the advance of knowledge as archaeology brought to light the existence of yet other peoples of like characteristics, and as it became possible to determine with greater scientific exactitude the typical or essential features which mark a language or a people or a culture as Semitic.

Before the eighteenth century all the languages and peoples of Asia had been referred to generically as Oriental. The affinity between certain Semitic languages had nevertheless been remarked from time to time, as when historical accident brought together those who spoke them. So for example the Jews in Spain, brought into contact with the Arabs who had penetrated into Europe across northern Africa, had been able to observe the similarity between their own language and that of the invaders.

Arabia, Syria-Palestine and Mesopotamia were, as has been said, the historical home of the Semitic peoples, and they occupied those lands solidly and continuously. That does not mean, however, that they did not spread beyond the boundaries of those lands, whether in incursions of greater or less extent and duration, or to establish themselves permanently.

A permanent establishment of Semitic peoples outside the Semitic area took place on the African coast over against the Yemen. Long before the beginning of the Christian era, various Arab tribes had begun to migrate thither, attracted by the natural wealth of the country, and had opened trading-stations there. Many ports so grew up along the coast of the Red Sea, while the immigrants also spread to the interior and established themselves there as settled colonists, imposing their rule on the native inhabitants. Such was the origin of the ancient state of Axum.

Among the migrations that were not destined to be lasting are to be numbered all the various attempts at military conquest, of which that of Islam was by far the most extensive. The subsequent decline of Moslem power and the splitting-up of the Arab Empire still left many Arabic, and hence Semitic, elements in the languages and in the blood of the peoples overrun by the tide of conquest.

Semitic populations spread beyond the homeland in yet another way: by colonization. The great colonizers among the Semitic peoples were naturally enough the people famous throughout antiquity for their maritime prowess, the Phoenicians. The foundation of bases at strategic points in the Mediterranean world was indeed necessary for the maintenance of their commerce; and so they founded colonies in Africa, in Spain, and in Sicily. The subsequent history of these colonies brought Semitic elements into the affairs of the European West even long after the power of Phoenicia itself had passed away for ever.

Finally, a diffusion of Semitic ethnic and cultural elements was brought about, at a period which lies outside the scope of this book, by the scattering of the Jews, which began even before the destruction of Jerusalem by the Romans, and has planted all over the world groups of Jews clinging tenaciously to their traditions.

The Semitic peoples are distinguished, as a group, from others by the possession of certain common characteristics of their own. These are mainly linguistic ones. Semitic languages have so much in common in their phonology, morphology, syntax and vocabulary, that their similarity can not be accounted for by borrowings in historic times, but only on the hypothesis of a common origin.

The phonology of the Semitic languages is characterized by a remarkably rich consonantal system, with many laryngeal, pharyngeal and uvular articulations, and with what are called "emphatic" consonants, whose articulation is accompanied by a constriction of the larynx. These typically Semitic consonants, which have practically nothing to correspond to them in the languages of Europe, may all be brought under the general heading of a shifting further back than in other languages of what may be called the "centre of gravity" of the system of articulation.

The vowel-system, on the other hand, is ralatively poor in phonemes. It is characteristic of most of the Semitic languages that the vowels are not written, but are supplied by the reader from the arrangement of the consonants alone. The vowels are written, however, in certain texts, to whose exact pronunciation especial importance is attached, such as the Hebrew Bible and the Arabic Koran.

The morphology is based on a system of "roots", the majority of which consist of three consonants. The basic meaning of the word is expressed by these consonants, while the addition of vowels, and also of consonantal prefixes, infixes and suffixes, determines the word's precise sense and function. For example, the three consonants *k-t-b* constitute a root, whose fundamental meaning is that of "writing". The root as such is a grammatical abstraction; words in actual speech are formed by the addition of vowels, of prefixes, infixes and suffixes. Thus, in Arabic, *kataba* means "he has written", *katab-ta* "thou hast written"; *kātib* is "writer", *kitāb* is "book"; *ma-ktab* is a "writing-place", that is, a "school"; and so on, for a wide range of verbal and nominal forms. Dictionaries of Semitic languages are arranged not in order of individual words, as are those of European languages, but in order of roots. So, for example, the word *maktab* will be found not under the letter *m*, but under its root *k-t-b*.

Semitic nouns were declined, but only a few of the Semitic languages have preserved the system of declension. The singular had a nominative in -*u*, a genitive in -*i*, and an accusative in -*a;* the dual a nominative in -*ā* and an oblique case in -*ay*; and the plural a nominative in -*ū* and an oblique case in -*ī*.

The use of the genitive case is characterized by what is called the "construct state" of the noun to which it is attached; this noun, preceding the word in the genitive, loses the definite article, and often suffers internal modification. For example, in Hebrew "the death", by itself, is *ham-māweth*, but if one adds "of the king" (*ham-melekh*) the resulting phrase "the death of the king" is *mōth ham-melekh*.

The Southern Semitic languages, that is, Arabic and Ethiopic, are characterized by a special type of plural-formation, that of what are called "broken" or "inner" plurals. Alongside the system whereby the plural is indicated, as is usual in European languages, by the ending of the noun, these languages form plurals also by means of an inner modification of the noun, generally a change in its vowels. Thus, for example, in Arabic, as has already been said, "book" is *kitāb*. The plural, "books", is *kutub*, formed by a change in the vowels only. This kind of plural represents as a matter of fact a collective, and this may account for the apparent singularity of the phenomenon.

26

The Semitic manner of word-formation will seem less strange to those who speak English than to those who speak, for instance, a Romance language; for in English we have such phenomena as the verbal forms "sing—sang—sung" and the noun "song", and even plurals formed in a similar manner, for instance, "man—men". Whereas, however, even in English such formation is restricted to certain words, in the Semitic languages it is normal. An interesting example is furnished by the English word "inch": this has been borrowed by Arabs, in its singular form: *insh*; but for its plural it has the form, which seems to the Arabs perfectly natural and obvious: *unush*.

The Semitic verb is characterized by a series of "themes" expressing derivatives of the basic meaning, and formed by regular modifications of the root; so are expressed for example an intense or repeated action, a causing-to-act, and the notions of passive, reflexive, reciprocal action. Semitic verbs are quoted normally not in the infinitive, though the English infinitive may be used in giving their meaning, but in the third person singular masculine of their perfect tense, since this is their simplest form. For example, the verb "to write" in Arabic would be given as *kataba*, though this word, as we have already seen, means in fact "he has written". By lengthening the first vowel we get *kātaba*, and this expresses reciprocal action, "to write to one another", "to correspond"; by prefixing *a-* and dropping the first vowel within the root we get *aktaba*, and this means "to cause to write". It is not difficult to see that many changes may so be rung on the consonantal root *k-t-b* with its general meaning of "writing".

Semitic languages have a system of conjugation quite different from that of Indo-European languages. They have properly speaking no "tenses" at all, that is, no forms distinctive of the present, past or future time of the action; they distinguish only what is called "aspect", that is they distinguish a state from an action, an activity (continuous or habitual) from a (completed) act. We may take as an example the system used in Arabic and the other Western Semitic languages. If the action, at the time referred to, which must be inferred from the context, is (or was, or will be, or for the writer's purpose is regarded as being) complete, as an accomplished fact, the "perfect" is used; this may correspond to an English pluperfect or past or perfect referring to a past act ("I had written", "I wrote yesterday", "I have already written"), or to a perfect or present referring to a future act ("I will come when I have written this letter", "He will find out when I write to him"), or to a future perfect ("I shall have written before then"). If on the other hand the action at the time referred to is not to be regarded as an accomplished fact, but as an incompleted or habitual or prospective action, the "imperfect" is used; this may correspond to an English continuous tense ("I am—was—will be writing") or to an expression of habitual action ("I used to write", "I write—wrote—will write every week"), or to one of envisaged action ("I shall write", "I was going to write").

Semitic syntax makes a characteristic distinction between what are called "verbal" and "nominal" propositions. In verbal propositions, which are the ordinary form of expressing an event or a stage in a narration, the verb is put in the forefront, and is followed by its subject; for example, the order of words is "said Zaid to his father", and not "Zaid said . . ."

In nominal propositions, however, the logical subject is put in the forefront, and the rest of the proposition constitutes a logical predicate saying something about that subject. Commonly, by an idiom found also in European languages, the verb "to be" is understood, for example "Zaid wise", meaning "Zaid is wise". The logical subject need not be the grammatical subject of the verb, however, but, after being enunciated, may be left "hanging in the air" from the point of view of normal Indo-European syntax, and followed by a verbal phrase with its own grammatical subject. Such constructions are to be found for instance in the Bible, not merely in the Hebrew, but carried into the Greek of the New Testament, for example: "he that overcometh, and he that keepeth my works unto the end, to him will I give authority over the nations" (Revelation 2, 26).

The sentence is in general simple in construction. Semitic languages do not favour subordinate clauses, preferring simply to juxtapose a series of propositions, leaving their relationship to one another, as conditional, final, causal or the like, to be gathered from the context. Even some of the clauses commonly classed as subordinate are not entirely so, being expressed without introductory "subordinating" particles. A typical example is furnished by Arabic "relative" clauses of the type "a book, we took it down, . . ." meaning "a book, which we took down, . . ." Very similar are what are called "circumstantial" clauses, for example: "shall I seek for you a god other than God, and He has favoured you above all creatures", meaning ". . . seeing that He has favoured you . . ." A striking example of this Semitic omission of subordinating conjunctions even in the Greek New Testament is S. Paul's exclamation, literally: "Thanks be to God that ye were servants of sin but became obedient . . .", where the English Revisers' text has, according to the sense, "thanks be to God, that, whereas ye were servants of sin, ye became obedient . . ." (Romans 6,17).

The Semitic linguistic peculiarities which have just been described are of course only typical examples from a much wider range; and they admit of exceptions. They suffice, however, as an outline of the distinctive features of the Semitic group as an individual linguistic family. The whole body of common elements may be organized in a theoretical reconstruction of a single original " Semitic", and this reconstruction brings out the close relationship to one another of the historical Semitic languages.

The latter may be classified in certain main groups, which offer a basis for the classification of the peoples who spoke them. The Semitic language-group of which we have the earliest documentary evidence is that of the Akkadians, that is, the Semitic peoples of Mesopotamia: Babylonians and Assyrians. A second group is formed by the languages called Canaanite because spoken in the region (comprising Palestine and part of Syria) which the Bible calls Canaan. Canaanite as a language-group has as complex a composition, and as dubious a claim to be regarded as a single individual unity, as have the Canaanites as a group of peoples. Hebrew belongs to this linguistic group. A third group is the Aramaic, a set of dialects first attested in Upper Syria, but later extending far into the surrounding regions. A fourth group is the Arabic, known to us before the time of Mohammed from a series of inscriptions principally from the Yemen, but having as its "classical" form the dialect of the Koran and subsequent Islamic literature. The fifth and last group is the Ethiopic, spoken by the Semitic colonists of Abyssinia; in ancient times Ethiopic was a single language; only in the middle ages, and so beyond the limits of this book, does it become a group by splitting up into clearly distinguished dialects.

We have described the geographical bloc inhabited by the Semitic peoples, and the common features of the languages which they spoke. The question still remains, however, to what extent we are justified in speaking of "Semitic peoples". In other words: the Semitic languages undoubtedly go together to form one distinct and united family; but can we say as much of the peoples who spoke them?

This question is not a simple one. Several scholars have maintained that the notion of "Semitic" as a class is justifiable only within the linguistic field, and that it cannot properly be applied to peoples or to forms of civilization; others have asserted the contrary, backing up their assertion by pointing to the "family likeness" distinguishable in the social and religious institutions of the Semitic-speaking peoples.

In order to clear up this matter, we must decide what constitutes a people. For modern ethnology, a "people" is an aggregate of persons, who, though they may differ in race and place of origin, are welded into a homogeneous unity by community of habitat, language, and historical and cultural tradition.

When we apply this definition to the Semitic-speaking peoples, we find, in addition to its obvious immediate applicability to each one of them individually, that there is no objection on geographical grounds to the homogeneity of the group as a whole, while there was never any objection to the recognition of a Semitic linguistic community; what remains to be seen is the applicability of the definition to historical and cultural tradition as a justification of the "Semitic" nature of the entire family.

We shall see in the next chapter how in historic times Semitic-speaking peoples have issued from the Arabian desert. Our historical sources record these migrations, and the economic and social conditions of the desert make them inevitable, leading as they do to a continual trend of nomadic pastoral tribes towards settlement in the more fertile regions around the desert, and the adoption of an agricultural mode of life. The Semitic-speaking peoples seem therefore to form one bloc not only by their being geographically assembled within the one area, and by speaking dialects of the one language, but also by sharing the one cultural and historical origin. Hence it seems justifiable not to restrict the expression "Semitic" to the linguistic field, but to speak of "Semites" and of Semitic peoples and culture.

An important distinction must however be made here: a people is not necessarily Semitic to the extent to which its language is Semitic. The desert-dwellers who occupied the surrounding territories imposed upon them their own language; but they mingled with the populations which they found in the lands they invaded, and took over to a large extent their culture. Hence the peoples that were so formed, while Semitic in language, and drawing for their culture upon the common Semitic inheritance, were independent ones, of which the Semitic element, though it might be the predominant and distinctive one, was not the only constituent. With the reserve, therefore, that this implies, we may call them "Semitic peoples", but it would be inaccurate to refer to their members indiscriminately as "Semites".

It remains true, however, that there was a real unity and community of tradition within the Semitic group of peoples, and for that reason a study of that group is not an arbitrary collection of elements only accidentally related, but a picture of a well-defined organic unity within the political and cultural history of the ancient Near East.

We now come to the racial question, and here it must be pointed out at the outset that this is one which does not affect the determination of the Semitic peoples as such: even the most compact and homogeneous of peoples may contain quite disparate racial elements. Moreover, there is no need even to discuss the theory, which belongs to the realms of now outmoded political propaganda rather than to serious scholarship, and which is justly discredited by anthropologists, of a "Semitic race" as a distinct race embracing all the Semitic-speaking peoples.

We may, however, examine the racial types to be found in the Semitic area. At the present day there are two predominant ones. In the first place we have the "oriental" or "Iranian" type, and in Arabia and parts of Palestine, Syria and Mesopotamia this is the only predominant one. It is distinguished by white (or sun-browned) skin, dark hair and eyes, strong growth of the beard and of the body-hair, middle stature, slim build, a long head with prominent occiput, a long face, a high strong nose, straight or convex, full lips, and a strong chin. In Palestine, Syria and Mesopotamia we find alongside this type another one, originating in the north, and called "Armenoid". This type is distinguished by dull-white skin, sturdily-built figure, a short lofty head with flat occiput, a strong and prominent nose with its base set high up, and thin lips. Certain elements of this latter type have come to be regarded as characteristic of the Jews.

These data are those of the present day. We have little evidence of the state of affairs in ancient times, but such evidence as we have points to the original prevalence over the whole Semitic area of the oriental or Iranian type, whereas the Armenoid type penetrated into the area only during the second millennium before Christ.

What conclusion is to be drawn from all this, as regards the present problem? In the first place, we have a contradiction of the theory of a racial group coincident with the Semitic linguistic group. On the one hand, the two racial types which we have described are not confined to the Semitic area; the oriental type extends to Iran and North Africa, and the Armenoid one to Anatolia and the Caucasus. On the other hand, they are not to be found in all Semitic areas; in Abyssinia the Ethiopians present a different racial type of their own.

What matters, however, for the question as we have put it is the racial status of the inhabitants of the Arabian desert, whence the Semites came; and here we find, as was only to be expected, in view of the isolation of the desert and the uniformity of its conditions, a remarkable racial homogeneity. It would seem, therefore, that though there is strictly no such thing as a Semitic race, yet the Semites were originally an ethnic group, and one whose cohesion is strengthened by homogeneity of race, within the wider "oriental" type.

CHAPTER THREE

THE PROLOGUE

HISTORY begins with the appearance of written documents, and our earliest such records of any Semitic people present it to us as an already individualized and differentiated unit in its own sector of the Semitic area. The various peoples have however enough in common to justify the hypothesis that they spread from an earlier common habitat to the lands which they occupy historically.

It is well to make clear the exact scope of this hypothesis and of its investigation. There is here no question of identifying an "original homeland" of the Semites. Attempts to do this have been made several times in the past, but any such investigation carries us back far beyond history, and its results can only be hypothetical and questionable. We must here limit ourselves to identifying the area whence there took place the historically known expansion of the Semites, without attempting to decide whether this was the area in which they first came into being as a people, or whether they had migrated thither in prehistoric times.

Even with this limitation the problem is not an easy one. The notion of a genealogical tree showing the progressive multiplication of peoples and tongues is no longer accepted without question. It is clear that in prehistoric times no less than in historic ones the relationships between peoples and languages may have been of a complex and shifting nature, which we are wholly unable to trace; and the idea of a process of progressive differentiation must be supplemented and corrected by that of fusion, whereby different dialectal or ethnical elements, thanks to political or cultural reasons, so far from developing away from one another, are brought together.

In spite of these reserves, however, the question of Semitic origins is one which may and indeed must be asked; but what has just been said must be borne in mind in answering that question.

One fact seems well enough established: so far as history shows us, Semitic migrations have had for their starting-point the Arabian desert. The only movements in the opposite direction are a few defensive ones of limited extent; and all the movements from the desert were movements of Semitic-speaking peoples. The fact that movements also took place from one part to another of the settled areas is no grounds for objection; it is obvious that the Semites, once they have penetrated from the desert into the settled areas, continue to take part in the historical movements which took place there, and that these subsequent movements are irrelevant to the question of Semitic origins.

It is important to note that historical documentation is not the only basis for the view that the Semites came from the Arabian desert. There is also the fact that the economic and social conditions of the desert are such that its nomadic pastoral inhabitants inevitably tend to overflow into the surrounding agricultural areas. This tendency is still to be seen in our own days, and since the conditions of the desert seem to have undergone no substantial change since the dawn of history, it is reasonable to suppose that it operated also in ancient times.

It is especially important in dealing with the present question to observe that in the whole of the Semitic area it is the Arabian desert that constitutes what ethnology and linguistics call a sheltered region. Of all the regions of that area it is the least open to communication, the least affected by what goes on around it. Such a condition makes for ethnical and linguistic conservatism; it is in such a region that we must expect to find the most archaic forms. The Arabic language fully confirms this *a priori* judgement;

and there is no reason to doubt its correctness in the ethnical sphere.

At this point it must be remarked that recently Professor Albright has put forward reasons for doubting that the camel, which is indispensable for life in the inner desert, was domesticated earlier than the first half of the second millennium before Christ. If these doubts are justified, what modifications do they impose on the thesis that the Semites came out of the desert? Not many, in my opinion: it would simply be necessary to suppose that they had inhabited only the outer desert, where a seminomadic life is possible without camels. It must be said, however, that those doubts are matters of controversy, and that there are indications of the existence of domesticated camels at an earlier date.

Arabia is not the only area that has been suggested as that whence the Semites came to their historical homelands; some have thought of Syria, others of Armenia, others of Africa; and an Italian scholar, Ignazio Guidi, has built up an interesting case, on linguistic grounds, for a Mesopotamian origin. It is difficult, however, to square such theories with the bulk of the historical and ethnological evidence; in the present state of knowledge we must admit, at least as a working hypothesis, that the area from which the Semites spread was the Arabian desert, and, more probably, its outskirts.

The conditions in which the ancient Semites lived are of notable importance for the interpretation of the whole subsequent course of their political and cultural history; they laid the foundation of the character of the Semitic peoples, and profoundly influenced their outlook and their behaviour.

Desert conditions, as we have already said, have changed but little from the earliest historic times down to our own day. Hence the data furnished by ethnological study of the Arabian desert-dwellers of today have much to contribute to our reconstruction of the past. We may draw also upon Arabic literature, which gives us ample descriptions of beduin life, and upon Hebrew literature, such as the book of Genesis, in which we see the transition taking place from nomadic to settled life.

Thanks to these various sources of information, we are enabled to form a clear enough picture of ancient Semitic social conditions. They were those of pastoral nomadism; full nomadism in the inner desert, if the domestication of the camel rendered such a manner of life possible, and partial nomadism, with herds of sheep and asses, nearer the outskirts of the desert. The process whereby semi-nomadic tribes attach themselves to settled ones is still to be seen in operation nowadays; sometimes the desert tribes have fixed bases to which they return in spring, when the sun begins to burn up the grass and dry up the wells of the moorland; sometimes they have no such bases of their own, but have arrangements with the settled tribes, whereby the latter give them grazing-rights in return for protection. The passage to settled life takes place when a semi-nomadic tribe, or part of it, gives up the practice of returning to the desert in winter, and settles down to agriculture in the fixed bases. This is on the whole a natural and peaceful evolution, but it may have episodes of violence, if the settled tribes are unwilling to come to an agreement, or when violent movements in the interior of the desert have repercussions on the outskirts.

The basic unit in the social organization of the nomads is the family. Though traces of a matriarchal structure are not lacking, the supreme authority is that of the father; inheritance is in the male line, and the sons, when they marry, mostly remain, with their wives, to swell the paternal household.

The nomads are in principle polygamous, but their polygamy is in practice limited by economic considerations, for it is not easy to maintain a large family in the desert, and the less encumbrances a man has, the better he can face life there. Historical legislation dealing with the family sanctions polygamy, but without showing it any especial favour; indeed, at times it sets limits to it.

The nomads choose their wives, preferably, within their own tribe, that is, endogamically. The force of tradition and the ideal of racial purity, which have so large a place in tribal life, cause the taking of alien wives to be viewed with disfavour. The book of Genesis, which moreover depicts a more highly-evolved situation, tells us of the grief caused to Isaac and Rebecca by Esau's taking Hittite wives (Genesis 26, 34-35); and when the question arises of the marriage of the younger son, Jacob, his father Isaac exhorts him to take a wife of his own people (Genesis 28, 1-2).

Above the family is the tribe, a collectivity composed of families united by bonds of blood-relationship and common interest, living together and migrating together. The need for security creates a strong feeling of solidarity, and this is one of the most characteristic features of nomadic society. In virtue of this solidarity, an offence against any member of the tribe is resented by the entire tribe, and the entire tribe shares in the duty of avenging it. The inexorable law of retaliation, "an eye for an eye and a tooth for a tooth", tempered only here and there by the possibility of "blood-money", has passed into much of the historical legislation of the Semitic peoples.

Property-rights are inevitably rudimentary and limited. It may be said with truth that the nomad carries all his property about with him. His own personal possessions are limited to the few weapons (lance, bow and arrows) which he needs for his personal defence. The very tent in which he lives is the common property of the family, and the pasture-lands are that of the tribe. The beduin have been described as aristocratic communists, a happy expression, for while the economic system, in which the notion of community prevails and that of private property is practically unknown, merits the name of communism, the social spirit, with its deep sense of personal pride, honour and tradition, gives these poor pastoral people a right to be called aristocrats.

Authority exists in the tribe only to a limited degree. There is no "government" in the proper sense of the word, but there is a chief, elected for his personal qualities by a council of elders. He is strictly *primus inter pares*; the limited power accorded him by the council is temporary and may be revoked. He acts as a judge, but only when the contending parties voluntarily submit their case to his judgement.

Looked at as a whole, the conditions of desert life are such as to create and foster an energetic spirit. The struggle for existence, the dangers and hardships imposed by nature, harden the character and quicken the faculties. Many times in the course of history, the struggles between the Semitic peoples and those about them take on the form of an opposition of fresh and lively forces to tired and decadent ones.

The conditions of social life did much to determine in their turn the manifestations of religious life. Here reconstruction is not easy, and takes us beyond the limits of Semitic religion into the vast problems of the origin and development of human religious institutions.

The Arabs of pre-Islamic times may be regarded in this respect, as also in that of their social life, as having preserved more faithfully than any other people the ancient Semitic conditions, just as they preserved with so little change the material conditions of desert life. Their polydaemonism, that is, belief in many local divinities, attached to trees, plants, rocks and water, must be very ancient, and typical of the nomadic way of life. The same may be said of the tribal gods, those peculiar to one or more groups, whose cult, thanks to the isolation of their worshippers, was rarely able to spread or to take root outside narrow limits. These deities had no fixed abode, just as their cult was inevitably lacking in fixed centres and sanctuaries; they were adored in various places, as the tribes moved about, and each one was regarded as bound to his own people, sometimes by ties of blood-relationship, as its supreme chief and judge. In certain cases some of these tribal deities attained a considerable importance, thanks to the ascendancy of the tribes to which they belonged; but their prestige was always dependent in that manner upon political circumstances.

There are many deities common to several Semitic peoples, but it is not always certain that such deities can be traced back to the primitive stage of Semitic religion, and for this reason we leave a more detailed discussion of them to the chapters dealing with the individual peoples. Here it must suffice to mention some of the most widely-recognized ones, namely El, perhaps originally the sky-god, Baal, perhaps originally the god of the fertilizing rain, and Astarte, perhaps originally the goddess of the morning-star (the planet Venus), but later identified with the Earth-Mother, an ancient divinity of the Near East. Other heavenly bodies too, the sun and the moon, must have had an ancient and widespread cult.

There has been discussion in several quarters of a supposed tendency towards monotheism, and in particular of the connection between such a tendency and the conditions of desert life. Such a hypothesis is an interesting one, but it is not easy to form any clear judgement as to its validity.

The forms of ritual in use among the Semites, even after their establishment in settled peoples, often betray their nomad origins. For example, the Hebrew Passover, later transformed by the Resurrection into the chief Christian feast, is characterized by the sacrifice of a lamb and the use of unleavened bread, both of which features go back to the conditions of nomad life, in which the use of unleavened bread was imposed by the perpetual state of movement, while the lamb represents the shepherd's offering to the divinity of the first fruits of their flocks. There was no need of temples or of altars; the worship of the gods had perforce to be such as could be carried on without the aid of those appurtenances which were ruled out by the conditions of nomadic life.

By the inevitable historical process of migration, Semites passed progressively to a settled manner of life. Attracted by the fertility of the lands round about, groups of beduin repeatedly left their desert in search of greater economic prosperity. They so came into contact with organized forms of settled society, and their adaptation to the new ways of life did not take place without conflicts and reactions reflecting the old independent nomad spirit.

The beduin immigrants found themselves among peoples with a centuries-old political organization of absolutist type, under despotic sovereigns in complete contrast with their own tribal chiefs, who were elected and might be deposed by the elders, and whose authority was in every respect dependent upon the will of the tribe. Hence, while the economic conditions of agricultural society offered advantages attractive enough to induce the beduin to change their way of life, its political institutions were not so acceptable, and were inevitably felt as a change for the worse, an imposition which was a heavy spiritual price to pay for material betterment; so that the newcomers often introduced into Near Eastern society a disruptive and subversive force.

The degree to which the nomad immigrants assimilated themselves to the settled conditions varies from people to people; while some, such as the Babylonians and the Assyrians, departed radically from their primitive ways of thought and of life, others, such as the Arabs and the Hebrews, preserved more tenaciously throughout their history traces of the old hostility to every form of absolutism.

Thus, when Israel was united into a kingdom, this centralization of authority met with strong opposition on the part of a section of the people, while by others it was merely tolerated as a necessary evil of alien origin. Throughout the history of the monarchy, moreover, the representatives of Jewish religion sought to limit and control royal authority; priesthood and prophecy bore to a certain extent the character of a reaction against absolute monarchy, and in this sense, of an expression of the ancient inheritance, a link with the beduin spirit of independence.

In a similar manner the history of the Arabs is marked by traits going back to the ancient democratic organization. In the early days, the Caliph retained to a great extent the characteristics of the tribal chief, ready to give audience to all comers, to consult with everybody, and to make his decisions with the wisdom and good sense which had won him his election. In the course of time authority became more and more absolute, and passed little by little into the hands of ministers. The Arab kingdom then became transformed into the supra-national Islamic Empire.

So it was that the ancient conditions of nomad life continued to influence and to guide the historic course of the political and cultural development of the Semitic peoples.

CHAPTER FOUR

THE BABYLONIANS AND ASSYRIANS

DISCOVERIES

THE earliest historically recorded movements of Semitic peoples were in the direction of the Mesopotamian valley; they are attested from the third millennium before Christ and continue to be reported from time to time subsequently; and they led to the formation of strong and extensive Semitic states.

Our knowledge of Mesopotamian civilization is a relatively recent acquisition. Until the middle of last century there was little direct knowledge of it at all; our information was limited to what could be gleaned from the Bible and from fragmentary travellers' tales, and it was practically accepted that the great empires of ancient Mesopotamia had disappeared for ever beneath the sands. Towards 1850 however, systematically organized excavation began to give brilliant results: among the first archaeologists to succeed on a large scale were Botta at Khorsabad and Layard at Nineveh. The remains of temples and of palaces, colossal statues, seals and inscriptions were brought to light in ever-increasing numbers as the explorations continued.

The difficulties that had to be overcome were manifold, especially in the early stages, the work of the investigators being rendered slow and precarious above all by the lack of funds and by the more or less open hostility of the local authorities. Not all the finds were able to reach Europe; some were engulfed in transit by the floodwaters of the Tigris, others were destroyed or thrown into the river by fanatical beduin, who opposed an

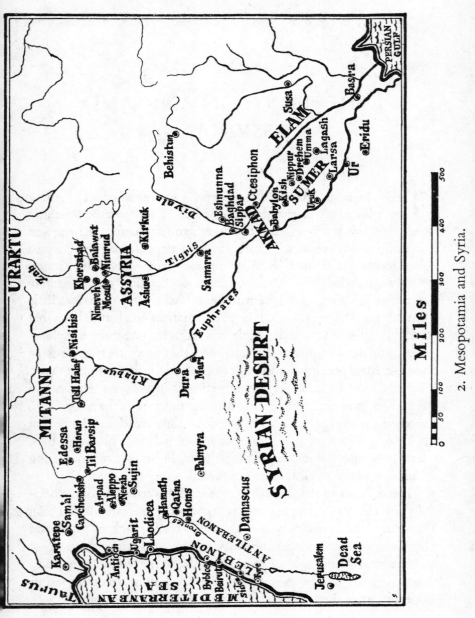

2. Mesopotamia and Syria.

armed resistance to what they regarded as the sacrilegious activity of the foreigners.

Nevertheless the importance of the results attained by the early excavations soon led European learned foundations to lend support and encouragement to the enterprise, so that work could be carried on more intensively and more efficiently. More and more ancient cities were brought to light, and with them, artistic monuments of a most imposing character, and an ever-increasing multitude of written records in the form of tablets of baked clay bearing inscriptions formed by wedge-shaped marks.

It is impossible to give here even an outline of the long and glorious history of assyriology. Suffice it to say that its most recent phases are among the most brilliant of all: at Mari the French archaeologist Parrot has discovered since 1933 (the excavations are still going on) a series of temples, palaces and statues, and more than twenty thousand tablets with economic and diplomatic texts; at Nimrud Professor Mallowan has reopened the excavations carried out there in the past, and has found new buildings and sculptures, and in particular a magnificent collection of ivory carvings; in the region of Kirkuk Professor Braidwood has identified a series of very ancient archaeological sites, which allow us to trace the essential lines of Mesopotamian prehistory.

The literary and artistic treasures of Mesopotamian archaeology have found their way into various great museums. The Louvre at Paris was first in the field, and has been able to build up a marvellous collection, representing all the epochs of Babylonian and Assyrian civilization. The British Museum in London is especially rich in documents from more recent times, but the ancient epochs are less fully represented. A first-class collection exists also at Constantinople, and of late years the Baghdad Museum has become exceptionally important.

The story of the interpretation of Mesopotamian documents

has an interest of its own because of the extreme difficulty of the system of writing used in them.

The decipherment began with the help of an inscription in three languages. The British consul at Baghdad, Rawlinson, who for a long time had been actively engaged in the search for Persian and Assyrian texts in Mesopotamia and on the Iranian plateau, discovered near Behistun in Persia an inscription in cuneiform but with three different kinds of script. One of the three texts was in the Persian character, and as progress had already been made in the decipherment of this, it was possible to use this text as a key to the interpretation of the most complicated of the three, which was in Babylonian.

Scholars attacked the problem from various directions, and various hypotheses were put forward; in 1857 an ingenious test brought out the amount of progress that had already been made. The London Asiatic Society had one and the same text translated independently by four assyriologists. The four versions were almost identical, so that it was plain that the translation was not a matter of capricious guesswork, and that Mesopotamian inscriptions had at long last yielded up their secret.

It soon became clear that in Mesopotamia the same system of writing had been used to write two completely different languages. One of these was not a Semitic one, and had been the language of the Sumerians, the people who inhabited Mesopotamia already in the third millennium before Christ; the other was the language of the Babylonians and Assyrians, the Semitic peoples who came in successive waves to take up their abode in the Mesopotamian valley.

Once the system of writing was sufficiently understood, the interpretation of Babylonian and Assyrian was facilitated by the knowledge of other Semitic languages. This part of the work was therefore not a very complicated matter; the language itself—Akkadian—is not so difficult, by comparison with other Semitic languages.

But though the language as such presented little difficulty, the system of writing, Sumerian in origin, was extremely complicated. Its signs had been evolved from drawings of objects. This kind of writing, which was also used by the ancient Egyptians, is called pictographic, because it designates an object by drawing a picture of it, or of some distinctive part of it. For example, to write "fish" one draws the outline of a fish, to write "ox", that of the animal's head and horns, to write "corn", an ear of corn. Actions may be expressed in a variety of ingenious manners; a drawing of the foot may mean "go", one of a man's head with the addition of the signs for bread or for water may mean "eat" or "drink", and so on. It is not easy, however, to make exact drawings, or to draw curved lines, on soft clay; hence the various drawings became reduced to stylized combinations of lines, representing only the idea that had been conveyed by their prototypes, and hence called ideograms.

The signs were originally arranged in vertical lines, beginning at the top right-hand edge of the tablet. In order to be able to write more conveniently, however, scribes adopted the custom of turning the tablet counter-clockwise through a quarter of a circle, so that the writing began at the top left-hand corner and was arranged in horizontal lines reading from left to right—as in English. Akkadian is one of the few Semitic languages written in this sense, as generally the opposite sense, from right to left, is preferred.

Restricted to these characters, however, cuneiform writing was seriously defective; it could not express, for example, many abstract ideas, or the various forms of the verb. In order to overcome this defect, it underwent a most important evolution: signs began to be used to represent not the idea of the pictures from which they were derived, but the corresponding phonetic entity. For example, the Sumerian for "milk" was *ga*; hence the sign for "milk" came to be used to write the syllable *ga*, independently of its meaning. Similarly other syllables could be written, and by their combination it was possible to write words (or parts of words, for instance in verb-forms) without recourse to ideograms. For example, in order to write the word *gaz*, meaning "to break", one wrote the sign *ga* ("milk") and then the sign *az* "bear", the animal), so giving *ga-az*.

The new form of writing so developed is called phonetic, and its invention was a great step forward in the direction of the simplification of the system of writing, as well as of its completeness. It still remained, however, an extremely difficult one. Ideographic values of signs did not entirely disappear, so that several signs may be interpreted either ideographically or phonetically, according to the context. Moreover, the majority of the ideograms, which are very numerous, consists of signs which may each have more than one phonetic value. For example, the sign derived from the drawing of the human foot may be read *gin* "walk" or *gub* "stand" or *tum* "carry", or in yet other ways. The correct reading of the signs was facilitated by the addition of determinatives (signs indicative of classes of meaning) or phonetic complements (giving part of the phonetic equivalent of the intended sense of the ideogram), and even in the absence of such aids one may go by the context; nevertheless it is easy to see how the decipherment of the inscriptions, especially if they have not been preserved in a good state of legibility, is often a real puzzle; the Mesopotamian system of writing is in fact one of the most difficult of those used in ancient times.

To us, who are accustomed to an alphabet composed of only a small number of signs, so impractical a system of writing is a source of perplexity. For all that, it is already a great advance in the art of writing. Other Semitic peoples, at a later date, were to give the world that most valuable invention, the alphabet.

HISTORY

The dominating factor in the history of Western Asia in

ancient times is the activity of the peoples of the Mesopotamian valley. Although their geographical situation made them gravitate naturally towards the Indian Ocean, they also exerted pressure on the one side towards the mountains of Iran and Armenia, and on the other towards the Mediterranean basin. The influence exerted by their armies and their forms of civilization in both of these directions was decisive in fixing the cultural and political balance of the Near East, of which Mesopotamia thus became a natural centre of reference.

The principal builders of Mesopotamian culture and history were two peoples of quite different origin, creators of the great artistic and literary monuments of that region: the Sumerians and the Akkadians. These two peoples lived so mingled together, that Mesopotamian culture and history is the product of a synthesis in which it is often impossible to distinguish clearly the two main components.

The Sumerians were probably already established from pre-historic times in southern Mesopotamia, where they early attained a high level of civilization. They began the excavation of canals, the rational exploitation of the soil, the erection of temples and of statues. Some of the latter give us an interesting picture of the Sumerian physiognomy, with its low receding brow, its prominent aquiline nose, and, at an earlier period, its long parted hair and square-cut beard; later we find clean-shaven heads and faces.

Sumerian culture left its immediate imprint also in Assyria, in Syria and in Egypt, but without any corresponding political expansion. Politically, indeed, the Sumerians were never able to build up any great power. They were organized in city-states, whose kings acted also as the priests and the representatives of the local deities. The history of the Sumerian cities is a continual tale of rivalries, in which the normal state of unstable equilibrium is now and again broken by the short-lived ascendancy of one city or another. The only state to attain to any notable pre-eminence was the one which king Lugalzaggisi succeeded in forming around his city of Umma. After having maintained his position of overlordship for many years, he was in the end conquered, towards the year 2350 B.C., by a Semitic dynasty.

Semitic groups had already been for some time in Mesopotamia, living in the country round the outskirts of the Sumerian cities, and keeping up their old traditions of pastoral life, before they appeared upon the political scene. Their first great self-affirmation as a political force was the victory whereby they overthrew the kingdom of Lugalzaggisi and established in its place the Semitic dynasty of Akkad. It must however be noted that princes with Semitic names are already attested some centuries earlier.

Recent studies, based on new documents now at our disposal (in particular, the Mari archives and the Khorsabad list of Assyrian kings) have led to the adoption of a new, shorter, chronology for the ancient Near East; the new chronology would put the dynasty of Akkad approximately between 2350 and 2150 B.C. This "short" chronology, associated with the names of Albright and Cornelius, is nowadays the most widely accepted one, but it is well to note that there are other systems, which would put the dates several decades earlier.

The founder of the dynasty of Akkad was the famous Sargon, of whom legend tells that he had been a gardener, and that as a baby he had been abandoned on the waters of the river, and thence miraculously rescued. Historical sources tell us that he extended his sway over the whole of Babylonia, Assyria and Syria, and even penetrated into Asia Minor. Under his rule the state took on a systematic and centralized organization, which was to serve as a model for the states to come after. We see here the appearance of the tendency to universal monarchy which will permeate the whole history of Western Asia up to the time of Islam.

Sargon's story, as we have seen, was soon enveloped in myth

and legend; but his actual achievements were such as to establish the Babylonian state firmly for a couple of centuries to come, until it was overwhelmed by the wild hordes of the Gutians, from the mountains to the east. The consequent prostration of Babylon beneath these invaders allowed the Sumerian cities to recover their strength once more. This was the period of the Sumerian prince Gudea of Lagash, a celebrated peace-loving sovereign, and a great builder of temples.

The Sumerian interlude was but of short duration; about the year 2000 B.C. a new Semitic people asserted itself both in Palestine and Syria, and at the same time in Mesopotamia. These were the Amorites, who founded a series of states and dynasties, including Mari on the middle Euphrates, and Isin and Larsa in southern Mesopotamia. Finally one of the Amorite dynasties attained pre-eminence, the so-called First Dynasty of Babylon (about 1830—1530 B.C.).

The sixth king of this dynasty was the famous Hammurapi, who lived about 1700 B.C. His reign marks another period of great prosperity. Politically, the power of Babylon extended over Assyria and part of Syria. In the religious sphere, Hammurapi was in particular responsible for the ascendancy of the god Marduk, who became the chief of the gods, and took over the attributes which had till then belonged to the old Sumerian divinities. Economically, Hammurapi reorganized and improved the country by means of a great development of agriculture and the digging of many new canals. On the bank of the most important of these he set up an inscription which reads: "Hammurapi is the people's plenty".

Literature also flourished greatly in this period; Hammurapi's chief title to fame, however, was the drawing-up of a code of laws, which enjoyed great celebrity throughout Mesopotamia. It was a codification of existing jurisprudence, embracing both Sumerian law and the juridical traditions of the Semitic peoples. Hammurapi is known to have shown an active interest in all that took place in his kingdom; his correspondence with his governors has been preserved to testify to the thoroughness of his personal management of state affairs.

The first Babylonian dynasty came to an end about 1530 B.C. An inroad of the Hittites, a people of Asia Minor, though itself of short duration, was the forerunner of a period of foreign domination. This was the period in which the "peoples of the mountains", of whom at least a part of the governing class was of Indoeuropean origin, were winning an ascendancy over the Near East.

No sooner had the Hittite raiders withdrawn, than another foreign domination established itself in Babylonia, that of the Cassites, a people from the east, which seems, judging by the names of its deities, to have contained Indoeuropean elements. They were present in Babylonia as the result of a long period of peaceful infiltration; but they now profited by the Hittite interlude to seize power for themselves, and they retained it for some centuries, until about 1160 B.C. The level of their civilization was much lower than that of the land they had conquered, and their domination brought about a sharp decline of Mesopotamian culture. They had however sufficient discrimination to appreciate the spiritual superiority of their subjects, and to make an effort to respect and adopt their ways; recently attention has even been drawn to a tendency in this period to restore Sumerian culture.

While the Cassites held sway in Babylonia, a Semitic nation was coming to the fore in northern Mesopotamia: the Assyrians. Assyria was above all a military power, and owed its prestige principally to its army's high degree of organization and of discipline.

The Assyrian state had at this period already been in existence for some centuries. An Akkadian dynasty founded by Ilushuma had been in power there at the turn of the nineteenth to the eighteenth century before Christ, and had been followed by the

Amorite dynasty of Shamshi-Adad I, whom the Mari archives show to have been a contemporary and a rival of Hammurapi. This older phase of Assyrian power had been followed by a long period of decline, culminating in the fifteenth century in reduction to the state of vassalage to the Hurrian state of Mitanni. Only in the following century, when Mitannian power was overthrown by the Hittites, was Assyria able to rise once more and to become by stages a great power. The independent policy inaugurated by king Ashuruballit culminated under Tukulti-Ninurta (1243—1207 B.C.) in the subjection of the whole region around Assyria and the laying waste of Babylon.

After Tukulti-Ninurta Assyrian expansion made no further advance until about a century later, when it was resumed with renewed vigour by Tiglath-pileser I, the founder of the New Empire, which extended to the Black Sea in the north, to the Mediterranean in the west, and to Babylonia in the south. After Tiglath-pileser, however, the pressure exerted by the Aramaeans held Assyria in check for another century and a half, after which there came another wave of conquest: Ashurnasirpal II restored the Empire to its old amplitude, and Tiglath-pileser III (745—727 B.C.) brought it to the height of its power. Assyrian policy was directed along three main lines: to the north the sovereigns aimed at securing control of the mountain passes and so rendering themselves safe from the threat of invasion from that quarter; to the west they subjected Syria and Palestine to tribute and brought under their own control the road to Egypt and to the sea; and to the south they treated their more highly civilized sister-state of Babylonia with a diplomatic prudence which finally brought Tiglath-pileser III to the throne of Babylonia also. This sovereign's policy was successfully continued by Sargon II, and when Esarhaddon even succeeded in conquering Egypt it seemed for a short period (671—653 B.C.) as if the millennial struggle between the two valley-powers had been brought to an end for ever. Ashurbanipal (668—626 B.C.), famous in legend as

Sardanapalus, was the last great sovereign of Assyria. His successors were soon to succumb before the onslaught of the Medes, who swept down from the Iranian plateau and in 612 captured and destroyed their capital, Nineveh. So perished the Assyrian empire, and its great palaces, along with the magnificent library which Ashurbanipal had patiently amassed for the glory of his nation, were swallowed up by the sands that were to keep their secret for thousands of years to come. So were fulfilled the words of the Hebrew prophets, who even at the height of Assyrian prosperity had not ceased to foretell the downfall of the mighty foe.

Babylonia, which after the Cassite period and several native dynasties had come to form part of the Assyrian empire, was enabled by the latter's decline to repair its own fortunes. In the conquest of Nineveh the Medes had as an ally the Babylonian general Nabopolassar, who founded in Babylon the Chaldaean dynasty (625—538 B.C.). With this dynasty power passed into the hands of the Aramaean element which for centuries had been penetrating progressively into Babylonia. Nabopolassar's son Nebuchadnezzar carried Babylonian conquest to the borders of Egypt, capturing and destroying in 586 Jerusalem, capital of the kingdom of Judah.

The Bible represents Nebuchadnezzar as a warrior. In his own land he earned lasting renown mainly for his peaceful works: temples, canals and roads were multiplied, and Babylon recovered her ancient splendour. His warlike exploits are recorded in the Babylonian chronicle (published in 1956 by Wiseman) and at the same time Xenophon and Herodotus report the construction of gigantic fortifications, including a huge wall which was to render Babylon impregnable.

All this was in vain. Cyrus and his Persians, who had succeeded the Medes in power in Asia Minor, soon turned their attention to Babylonia, where political decadence had been accompanied by a growth of the power of the priesthood of Marduk. The last sovereign of the Chaldaean dynasty, Nabonidus, was until recently looked upon as an antiquarian, unaware of the gathering tempest; but now he is rather regarded as the author of a last effort to restore the most ancient forms of Babylonian worship. The Persians, favoured by the priesthood of Marduk, did not give him time to do so. War began in 539, and when the great wall fell and Cyrus made his entry into Babylon, the latter's power was at an end for ever.

Regarded as a whole, the ancient history of Mesopotamia is marked by a noteworthy unity, in the sense that strong political forces were able to arise there and expand from there as their centre. The states so formed, however, were themselves complex in their composition. In the third millennium the Sumerian population, hitherto undisputed masters, come into contact with immigrants and, while gradually ceding supremacy to the new-comers, profoundly influence their culture and civilization. In the second millennium supremacy is in the hands of the Semitic peoples, passing with various vicissitudes from the south to the north, from Babylonia to Assyria, while outside elements penetrate periodically into the valley. The first millennium, after the apogee of Semitic power in the north, sees its progressive decline in the face of non-Semitic invaders. Repeatedly the latter sweep down from the mountains, and constantly the valley-dwellers turn their attention to the mountains in the effort to secure themselves against this menace. Those whom nature most favoured were the victors; by about 500 B.C. the independent history of Mesopotamia comes to an end, and henceforth political power is centred elsewhere, and Mesopotamia is but an element on the outskirts of the struggles of other powers.

RELIGION

Mesopotamian civilization was of a highly-developed type, differing notably both from the common Semitic heritage and from the civilization of other Semitic peoples. When the Semitic immigrants came into the Mesopotamian valley they were confronted by an established and individualized historical culture, and though they had their own cultural contribution to make, bearing the marks of their original conditions, they inevitably assimilated themselves more and more to their new environment. This meant that they receded further and further away from the conditions of life and culture of other Semitic peoples, none of whom, except perhaps the Ethiopians, inserted itself into an environment geographically and historically so different from that from which it came.

The most typical feature of Babylonian and Assyrian civilization, as compared with original Semitic institutions, is its transition from nomadism to settled life. The historical and cultural conditions of the Semitic peoples were profoundly modified by the mere fact of the fixation of the fluctuating state of their civilization when they settled down in fixed abodes, while at the same time the forms of their adaptation to their new environment were determined by their contacts with other peoples.

The non-Semitic people with whom the ex-nomads chiefly mingled in Mesopotamia was that of the Sumerians, whose civilization had attained a level far higher than that of the newcomers. Absorption by the latter of Sumerian elements was so constant and so widespread that many sectors of Babylonian and Assyrian culture depend directly upon such elements. Our knowledge of Sumerian texts and our ability to interpret them are but of recent date; the more we learn from these texts, the clearer it becomes how many of the traditions and conceptions of the Akkadians were not purely their own, but the product of a new synthesis of Sumerian elements. It is true that the Akkadians brought to the process of assimilation a spirit and an outlook of their own; but, as Rome with respect to Greece, so they were under the spell of the more exalted and original civilization of the older people.

Babylonian and Assyrian civilization, when once it had come into being as a result of this complex process of assimilation, exercised in its turn a far-reaching influence on all the regions round about it, and Mesopotamia became a cultural centre from which were propagated cosmological, mythological and scientific conceptions. A considerable part of the literature and of the customs of the other Semitic peoples is a more or less immediate echo of the voice of Mesopotamia. Nor were Mesopotamian ideas confined to the Semitic world; they penetrated into Asia Minor and reached even Greece. Modern scholarship is showing ever more clearly how Greek civilization, original as it is as a whole, is indebted for many of its conceptions to the peoples of Mesopotamia.

The aspects under which Babylonian and Assyrian civilization is to be considered are religion, literature, jurisprudence and art. These are not entirely distinct and separate entities, but interpenetrating one another and form together a complex unity. This is a normal phenomenon in the ancient Near East, where the distinction between these aspects of culture is not so clearly drawn as it is in the modern world. No distinction is made, for instance, between sacred literature and profane, between civil law and religious law.

In every department of human life religion is the ruling factor. As is the case throughout the ancient Near East, literature, law and art are envisaged in Mesopotamia only in connection with religious motives, and these motives penetrate every manifestation of life and so make up the innermost substance of that life. This is perhaps the most distinctive feature of ancient Near Eastern civilization. Human values are epitomized in religion; for independent philosophical speculation and artistic creation we must await the coming of the Greeks.

The syncretistic character of Mesopotamian civilization is nowhere more evident than in its religious institutions. Its

Semitic gods were largely Sumerian deities, taken over, with modifications, by the victorious invaders: a process which repeats itself often enough in the course of history. Moreover, the Babylonian and Assyrian divinities themselves subsequently fused and interacted with one another with the changing of the times and of the Mesopotamian political situation.

Akkadian religion is richly polytheistic. The characteristics of its gods are of like kind with those of human beings, and differ only by greater perfection and absoluteness. The gods dress like men, but their garments are even more sumptuous than those of earthly princes, and emit a dazzling brightness. They have families and weapons, and their strife is like the strife of men, but of course on a much grander and more terrible scale. Such a conception of the gods is closer perhaps to that of the Homeric poems than to that of the Semitic religions in general, but, as has already been said, the part played in all this by Semitic elements is doubtful, and certainly not large.

The supreme triad of the Mesopotamian pantheon was made up of heaven, air and earth, personified respectively by Anu, Enlil and Enki (Ea). Another triad was furnished by the heavenly bodies: the sun, the moon and the planet Venus (the "morning star"). As religion evolved, every god had his own star; and the worship of the stars increased with the advance of astrology.

Another nature-god was Adad, who represented the storm, whether in the milder and beneficent forms of rain and flood, which gave life to plants, or in the violent and destructive forms of lightning and hurricane, which robbed man of the fruits of his patient labour. Fire likewise was adored, in the person of the god Nusku.

In accordance with a conception belonging, as we shall see, to many peoples of Western Asia, the natural cycle of plant life, and the fertility of the earth, were venerated in the first place in a female divinity, Ishtar, who symbolized Mother Earth. The worship of this goddess was of great importance both within and beyond the frontiers of Mesopotamia, and a whole series of myths grew up around her. To her, as goddess of love, was dedicated the practice of ritual prostitution, which was widely diffused in connection with the fertility-cult. She presided also over war and battle.

With her was associated the young god Tammuz, whose nature was at once divine and mortal. He died and was reborn year by year, typifying the death and rebirth of plant-life. A myth rich in religious and poetical significance relates how the goddess Ishtar went down to fetch him from the abode of the dead.

Both Babylonia and Assyria had another kind of god, national in character, whose importance was naturally bound up with the political situation. In Assyria Ashur was such a god, and in Babylonia the celebrated Marduk, who attained predominance with the dynasty of Hammurapi. The traditions concerning the origin and ordering of the world were transferred to him, and all the other gods were represented as his subordinates and helpers in the gigantic task of creating and governing the universe.

The daily life of the Babylonians and Assyrians was perpetually overshadowed by the fear of demons. These were strange beings, able to take on any shape, to penetrate into whatsoever body, and to move unseen in every place. Generally they preferred deserted and dark places, ruins, cemeteries, and every other kind of fear-inspiring locality. They manifested their presence by animal noises, which in lonely spots inspired especial terror.

Mesopotamian art, faithfully reflecting the life of the people, abounds in representations of demons, commonly with human bodies and animal heads, or combining parts of various animals into a terrifying whole.

The demons were for the most part evil spirits who came up from beneath the earth; some were the ghosts of the unburied dead, who wandered restlessly from place to place and avenged themselves for their unhappy fate by attacking mankind and multiplying calamities.

The most striking feature of Mesopotamian religious psychology with regard to demons is that man was regarded as practically defenceless against them. Even one who led a blameless life and offended none of the gods might always be subjected to the machinations of a malevolent sorcerer, or come involuntarily into contact with some impure being or thing: man could be the innocent victim of evil forces. So deeply pessimistic an outlook points to the great weakness of moral conceptions, and the absence of a belief in just retribution in a future life for the deeds of this one.

Nevertheless, the most natural way for a demon to gain entrance into a man was through sin. The sin might be one of many kinds: failure to observe religious ceremonial, as well as theft or murder. No distinction was made between moral and ritual offences; all were put into the same category, thanks to the dominant role played by religious conceptions in the whole organization of everyday life.

When a man sinned, he was abandoned by the god under whose protection he lived, and the way was thus left open for the demons, who seized their opportunity to enter the man's body. Their presence at once made itself felt in various disagreeable phenomena: noises in the house, gusts of wind, terrifying visions.

The most usual manifestation of demoniac possession was however illness. The demon most feared by the peoples of Mesopotamia was perhaps the fever-demon, with his lion's head, ass's teeth and panther's limbs; his voice was as the voice of the leopard and the lion, his hands grasped terrible serpents, and a black dog and a pig nibbled at his breasts. Thus a sick man was a guilty man, and his sickness was due to the presence of a demon.

Starting out from such premises, Mesopotamian medicine naturally concluded that the curing of a disease consisted in the expulsion of the demon. For this purpose there was a detailed and complicated procedure. The sick man must in the first place identify the demon responsible for his malady. Here tradition came to his aid; the names of the demons that took up their residence in the various parts of the body had long been known, beginning with the *ashakku*, the demon of the head, who caused the headaches so much redoubted by the peoples of Mesopotamia. If the identity of the demon remained uncertain, recourse was had to a precautionary expedient: the sick man pronounced a long confession of possible sins, so as to make sure of mentioning the one he had committed.

It was next necessary to drive out the demon, and this was carried out by a priest who specialized in this procedure, by means of the series of exorcisms and magical operations required by the case.

The priest who specialized in assisting the sick in this manner was the exorcist (*āshipu*). A Babylonian bronze amulet has come down to us bearing a curious picture representing an exorcism. On the back of the amulet is depicted the demon, seen from the back, with his animal wings, limbs and head. The monstrous face projects over the front of the amulet, on which are pictures representing a series of scenes. The top row shows us, under the symbols of the gods, the seven fever-demons; in the middle row we see the sick man lying on his bed, surrounded by the priests in their vestments; while the bottom row contains a lively scene showing the demon cast out from the man's body and in full flight.

The exorcisms consisted in the recital of magic formulas accompanied by ritual actions. The ceremony opened with a prayer to the gods, describing the wretched state of the sinner, who begged for forgiveness. The sick man was sprinkled with holy water; pieces of meat were thrown, in order that the demon might seize them and so loose his hold on the patient's body.

All this shows how widespread was the use in Mesopotamia

of spells and magic. As an example we have the cure for a scorpion-bite: this began with the recital of spells over the part affected; then the patient took in his mouth seven grains of pure wheat along with mountain-herbs, and chewed all this; then he went and plunged himself seven times in the river, spitting out into the water on the seventh immersion the chewed pulp.

A second type of priest (bārū) had the charge of divination, that is to say, the art of interpreting and predicting the will of the gods which decided the outcome of earthly affairs. This further priestly function—and it was not the least of them—shows how highly-developed was the priestly organization and how great the influence of the priesthood on the life of Mesopotamia.

Divination was principally carried out by the examination of the liver of animals. The Babylonians and Assyrians attached a particular importance to this organ, and a whole branch of science was devoted to its study. Clay models have been found with the detailed indication of all the regions of the liver, and observations as to the meaning of each sector. If for example a king wanted information about the future, he called in the diviner-priest, who sacrificed an animal, usually a sheep, and made answer to the king according to the indications he read in the liver.

The other internal organs of animals were likewise studied in connection with the art of divination. Other objects of similar observation were the flight of birds, the appearance and behaviour of certain animals, and the birth of children. It was said, that if a newborn child lacked the right ear, this portended the downfall of the state, whereas if it lacked the left ear, this was a sign that the gods had heard the king's prayers, and that he would have victory over his foes. Almost every animate or inanimate object that fell within the range of man's observation might thus furnish matter for divinatory research.

Another form of divination was astrology. The movements of

the heavenly bodies, their meetings, their colour, all provided grounds for the prognostication of coming events, which in the mind of the Mesopotamian peoples were bound up with celestial phenomena. The whole of a man's life, for example, depended on the particular position of the heavens at the moment of his birth.

Observation of the heavens led to a great development of astronomical lore in Mesopotamia, especially during the Chaldaean period. We have many tables of astronomical data, which give proof of a most extensive knowledge of astral phenomena. The Babylonians possessed from the earliest times proper observatories, set on the summits of temple towers; they measured the courses of the stars with water-clocks, and kept an accurate record of the movements of the sun and moon, of which they were able to predict the eclipses by the seventh century before Christ. The names which they gave to the constellations were later taken over by the Greeks, who were indebted to Babylonia for a great part of their astronomical knowledge. Astronomy provided the basis for the calendar, formed of twelve lunar months.

The measurement of the apparent distances between the stars, and other astronomical calculations, some of considerable complexity, show an advanced knowledge of mathematics. The Mesopotamian peoples knew both a sexagesimal and a decimal system. They could add, subtract, multiply, divide, raise to powers and extract roots, and solve complex equations; in geometry they could measure areas and volumes.

This body of astronomical and mathematical knowledge undoubtedly constitutes one of the greatest contributions made by the Mesopotamian peoples, especially the Babylonians, to the history of civilization. Their development of these sciences was intimately connected, as we have seen, with their religion, and more particularly with the art of divination.

In addition to the exorcist and diviner there was the priest (kalū) charged with the carrying out of funeral ceremonies and the singing of dirges. The dead were buried in earthenware coffins or in reed-mats, and alongside them were laid various objects and provisions.

This custom corresponds to the Mesopotamian peoples' conception of what lay beyond the grave. This is a point of especial interest, inasmuch as it attests a belief in life after death, but without bringing out the idea of retribution for good and evil, and offers in general a negative and pessimistic impression of the life to come.

After death, it was believed, a man's soul passed through the tomb and descended into the underworld (*arallū*). This was a great city shrouded in dust and darkness. There the dead led a sad and gloomy life, drinking dirty water and eating dust. Their lot might be alleviated only by the offerings made by friends and relatives still living. Those who were neglected, along with the unburied, wandered restlessly about and returned from time to time to earth to trouble men in the guise of evil spirits. Only a few hints are to be found in Mesopotamian literature of any difference in the lot of the righteous and of the reprobate; thus we are told, for example, of the existence of an island of the blessed, to which a very small number of chosen ones were brought by the gods, who first rendered them immortal.

Mesopotamian ritual was extremely complicated, with a mass of rigidly and minutely determined details. This indicates the extent of the development of religious formalism, and at the same time the absolute supremacy of religion over every other aspect of social life.

The commonest and most usual of religious ceremonies was that of sacrifice, which might be offered for a variety of ends: in expiation of sin, in order to win the favour of a god, for the consecration of a new temple or a new statue, and so on; all this in addition to the ordinary sacrifices which were offered daily in the temples at appointed times.

The offerings consisted for the most part of animals and of

liquids. The animals most commonly offered were lambs and kids, the liquids wine, beer, milk, honey and oil. The sacrificial victim or other offering was set upon an altar before the statue of the god or goddess, and the ceremony began with prayers accompanied by ritual actions and sprinkling with holy water. Certain portions of the offerings, reserved to the divinity, were burned (or poured out in libations) in his or her honour, others formed the share of the priests, and the rest was given back to the person making the offering. It seems that there were dishonest priests who made a comfortable profit for themselves by substituting victims of inferior quality for those brought to them for sacrifice. The temples received great quantities of goods of various kinds, the administration of which was a complicated matter, as is to be seen from the account-books which have been found.

Ritual meticulousness is reflected also in the sacred calendar, which was likewise regulated by a host of detailed prescriptions. There was a general division of the days of the year into propitious and unpropitious, and the performance of various public and private acts on given days was authorized or prohibited in accordance with this division.

The feasts of the religious year were those of the gods, in which men joined with rejoicings and with ritual. Most important were the feasts of the patron deities of the various cities, and outstanding among these was the New Year celebration at Babylon. This included a solemn ceremony of humilation of the king. Huge masses of pilgrims flocked to the capital from all around, and the god was regaled with sacrifices and men with banquets. Prayer after prayer went up to Marduk, supreme god of the city and of the whole region ruled by the first dynasty of Babylon. On that day there took place the solemn determination of the destinies of the state for the whole year which it inaugurated.

Prayer was accompanied by a variety of gestures. It was usual to pray standing upright before the deity with the right hand raised. The custom of praying with open palms outstretched towards the deity seems to be of Semitic origin. There were prayers for public and prayers for private use; the latter were naturally couched in more detailed and personal terms, and the former in a more general and formal style.

LITERATURE

Babylonian and Assyrian literature differs notably both in character and in subject-matter from that of the other Semitic peoples. Mythology, so scarce among these in general, flourished luxuriantly in Mesopotamia, where an outstanding poetical literature is devoted to recounting the adventures of gods and heroes.

This contrast with other Semitic literature is however more apparent than real. The greater part of Akkadian mythology is simply a new redaction of Sumerian traditions, which in this way constitute the real foundation of Mesopotamian literature. The Akkadians had a great respect for the traditions of their predecessors, whose culture they took over; and they saw nothing to object to in the re-editing of other people's works. It may be said, indeed, that the notion of literary proprietorship was totally alien to the mentality of the ancient Near East, including Mesopotamia. Even the author's name was a matter of no importance, so that literary production was for the most part anonymous.

Force of tradition played a large part in literature, and fixed its conservative, indeed static nature. The ancient compositions were regarded as paragons which could not be improved upon, and consequently each generation of artists aspired above all to assimilate and reproduce their characteristics. It is interesting to remark that authors did not hesitate to reproduce several times in the course of the same work an image or a passage which they found satisfactory. Conversations or messages, for example, are reproduced in full each time they are referred to. It may be said in passing that this fact is nowadays a great help in the reconstruction of fragmentary texts.

The principle of repetition rules also the poetic form, whose distinctive regular periodicity is neither marked by rhyme nor measured by rhythm, but is constituted by the succession of balanced phrases, that is, by a repetition of ideas, whether the parallelism be that of equivalence or similarity, or that of contrast.

To sum up, there is a tendency to over-standardization, to the repetition of accepted types and schemes; so far from departing from the beaten track in an effort at self-expression, the artist tends to hide his own personality behind traditional forms; art is solemn and impersonal, conservative to the point of being static.

The great religious epics which recount the Mesopotamian myths of the gods reveal a preoccupation with the first origins and last destiny of mankind; for they deal in great part with the creation of the universe and with what lies beyond the grave.

The creation-myth is set forth in a long Akkadian poem referred to as *Enūma elish*, which are its opening words, meaning "When on high". The Akkadian redaction of this epic goes back to the time of the first dynasty of Babylon, and aims at glorifying Marduk as highest of the gods and creator of the universe.

In the beginning, says the poem, there was nothing save a great waste of waters, personified by two deities, one male, Apsu, and one female, Tiamat. This couple had a numerous progeny of gods, who before long rebelled against their parents. Apsu was slain, but Tiamat continued the struggle, spawning forth in her defence a host of hideous monsters with poison-fangs: the Viper, the Dragon, the Great-Lion, the Mad-Dog, the Scorpion-Man, the Lion-Demons, the Dragon-Fly, the Centaur.

Faced with this threat the gods elected as their leader and champion one of their own number, the young god Marduk; and he made his dispositions for the encounter with Tiamat:

"He fashioned a bow, and made it his weapon,
Fitted to it the arrow, and fixed its string.
He lifted the mace, and took it in his right hand,
Bow and quiver he hung at his side.
Lightning he set before him,
With a blazing flame he filled his body.
He made a net to enfold Tiamat;
The four winds he took that nothing of her
    might escape,
The South Wind, the North Wind, the East Wind,
    the West Wind.
At his side he set the net, the gift of his father,
    Anu.
He made Imhullu, the Evil-Wind, the Tempest, the
    Hurricane,
The Fourfold-Wind, the Sevenfold-Wind, the
    Ruinous-Wind, the Matchless-Wind;
He sent forth the winds he had made, the seven
    of them;
To stir up the inside of Tiamat they rose up
    behind him.
The lord raised up the cyclone, his mighty weapon;
He mounted the storm-chariot, irresistible,
    terrifying.
He harnessed and yoked to it a team of four,
The Destroyer, the Relentless, the Trampler-down,
    the Swift.
Sharp were their teeth, bearing poison;
They were trained to wreak havoc, had learned
    to lay low . . . .
With an armour of terror he was clad,
In a fearsome halo his head was enwrapped.
The lord went straight forth and went on his way,
Towards the raging Tiamat he set his course.

In his lips he held an amulet of red paste,
While in his hand he grasped a plant to destroy
poison . . .
Tiamat cried out aloud in fury,
Her legs trembled to their roots;
She recited a charm, and cast her spell,
And the gods of battle sharpened their weapons.
They joined issue, Tiamat and the wise among the
gods, Marduk;
They went to battle, they came near for the struggle.
The lord spread out his net to enfold her;
The Evil-Wind, which followed behind, he let loose
before her;
When Tiamat opened her mouth to destroy him,
He sent in the Evil-Wind, so that she could not
close her lips.
The raging winds filled her belly,
Her body was distended and she gaped her mouth.
He loosed an arrow, which tore her belly,
Cut through her insides, and split her heart."[1]

Having defeated in this wise the monster-goddess of the waters,
Marduk split her body in two with his sword, and fashioned
from one of the two parts the vault of the heavens, and from the
other the earth, so dividing the waters into those above and those
below the firmament. This last detail was called for by the
accepted explanation of rain as the overflowing of waters upheld
by the sky.

Having so formed heaven and earth, Marduk next set the stars
in the heavens. Here there follows a long lacuna; the missing
portion of the text most likely dealt with the creation of plants
and animals. The next legible portion of text shows us Marduk
taking earth and mixing it with the blood of the god Kingu,

_____
[1] *Enūma elish*, Tablet IV, lines 35—103, passim.

who had been slain in the battle, and fashioning of it man, to be the servant of the gods. When the work of creation was completed, the gods celebrated the triumph of Marduk, saluting him with fifty titles of honour.

This epic is in great part a compilation of Sumerian themes, applied to the new god whom the Babylonian dynasty imposed upon Mesopotamia. It may also embody a nature-myth, in which Marduk's victory over Tiamat symbolizes that of the sun in springtime over the storms of winter; it certainly expresses a fundamental notion of the ancient Mediterranean world: the victory of cosmos over chaos, creation seen as the reducing to order of a primal disorder.

The theme of the cycle of the seasons is more clearly recognizable in another myth, one of those treating of what lies beyond the tomb, namely the tale of Ishtar's descent into the underworld. The goddess of love goes down to *arallū* and demands to be announced to its queen, Ereshkigal. Her way into the queen's presence takes her through seven portals, and in order to pass through each one she is obliged to lay off one of her seven garments. When she reaches the queen the latter greets her by casting upon her sixty diseases. Meanwhile upon earth the absence of the goddess of love has brought to a stop all reproduction of life, and the gods in their anxiety send to Ereshkigal to beg her to release Ishtar. After being sprinkled with the water of life, Ishtar makes her way back to earth, recovering her garments as she passes once more through the seven portals; and with her return life is renewed upon earth.

Another myth of the Beyond is that of Nergal and Ereshkigal. The queen of the underworld, being unable to attend in person a feast of the gods, sends her minister Namtar to claim her share of the banquet. He is received with honour by all the gods except Nergal, who will not rise out of respect for him. Ereshkigal bids Namtar bring the recalcitrant god down to the underworld. Nergal does descend thither, but he overcomes the guards, seizes Ereshkigal by the hair, and drags her from her throne. She now begs for mercy and offers to take Nergal as her consort. The god accepts this offer and so becomes king of the underworld. This story seems to have arisen in order to justify the attribution to Nergal of sovereignty over the underworld; as in other cases, a mythological foundation is supplied.

One of the hero-myths stands out above the rest; it spread beyond the boundaries of Mesopotamia into the legends of the peoples round about. This is the Gilgamesh-myth, probably even more ancient than *Enūma elish*.

Gilgamesh is man seeking immortality. The epic is remarkable for the relative subjectivity and modernity of its attitude to life, which is fundamentally a bleakly pessimistic one: not even the heroes can escape death, and "the paths of glory lead but to the grave". The story told by the poem may not be entirely mythical. Its hero is represented as a king of Uruk, and there really was a Gilgamesh king of Uruk, whose adventures, coloured by legend, may have given rise to the myth.

Gilgamesh was the man who had seen all things, who knew hidden mysteries and had discovered the secret of wisdom; but he oppressed his people, and the gods wished to set up a rival against him. No man living was a match for him, so the gods created such a man, and gave him the name Enkidu. After various adventures, however, the two heroes became friends, and together accomplished fearsome exploits. After their victory over the dreadful monster of the cedar-forest, the goddess Ishtar herself was struck with admiration for Gilgamesh, and offered to make him her husband. This offer the hero rejected and, careless of the goddess's wrath, taunted her with her many cruel amours. This singular courtship is related as follows:

"He washed his grimy hair and polished his weapons,
He cast his locks upon his shoulders;

He took off his soiled clothes and put on clean,
Clad himself in his tunic and fixed his belt.
When Gilgamesh had put on his tiara,
Great Ishtar set eyes on his beauty:
Come, Gilgamesh, be thou my lover!
Grant me the gift of thy love,
Be thou my husband and I will be thy wife.
I will harness for thee a chariot adorned with lapis-lazuli
    and gold,
With golden wheels and with horns of precious stone.
Thou shalt harness to it storm-demons for horses,
Amid the fragrance of the cedars shalt thou enter our
    house!
And when thou enterest our house,
The threshold and the dais shall kiss thy feet.
Before thee shall bow down kings, governors and princes,
The produce of mountain and of plain shall they bring
    to thee as tribute.
Thy goats shall cast triplets, thy sheep shall bring forth
    twins,
Thy pack-ass shall surpass the mule,
The horses of thy chariots shall win fame for their
    racing,
The oxen beneath thy yoke shall know no rival.
Gilgamesh opened his mouth
And said to great Ishtar:
But what must I give thee, if I take thee in marriage?
Am I to give thee oil and garments for thy body,
Bread and victuals,
Eood for thy godhead,
Drink for thy queenship?
What do I gain from marriage with thee?
Thou art a door that withstands not the wind and the
    storm,

A palace which the heroes destroy.
Whom of thy lovers hast thou loved for ever?
Who of thy swains has been pleasing to thee always?
Come, I will tell thee the tale of thy lovers.
For Tammuz, the lover of thy youth,
Thou hast ordained mourning year after year.
Thou didst love the shepherd-bird of dappled plumage;
And smote him and broke his wing.
Now doth he sit in the groves and cry "My wing!".
Thou didst love the lion, marvellous in strength,
And didst dig for him seven pits and yet seven.
Thou didst love the stallion, splendid in battle,
And didst ordain for him whip, spur and lash;
Seven leagues didst thou bid him run,
And made him muddy the water ere he drinks.
For his mother, Silili, thou didst ordain mourning.
Thou didst love the shepherd of the flock,
Who ever gathered coals for thee
And daily slaughtered kids for thee;
Thou didst smite him and turn him to a wolf,
His own sons now hunt him down,
His own dogs snap at his legs.
If thou love me, thou wilt treat me like them."[1]

Gilgamesh's soul is next thrown into tumult by the sickness and death of Enkidu. He realizes that he himself must die some day. A prey to irresistible terror, he flees from place to place over the countryside. Why must man die? Not even Gilgamesh can fathom this mystery. He resolves to go to an old sage named Utnapishtim, to whom the gods have given the gift of immortality, and ask him the secret of life and death.

The journey is long and difficult. Crossing the waters of death, the hero at last reaches the old man's abode and tells him of his

---

[1]Gilgamesh, Tablet VI, lines 1—78, passim; the text is in places mutilated and uncertain.

trouble: in vain has he accomplished so many deeds of prowess; all joy is now at an end for him, sorrow has brought him down. The ancient replies bitterly: do man's works endure for ever? Love and hatred soon come to an end, the river rises but to fall again. Life and death are determined by the gods; but the gods do not tell us the day of our death.

The old sage had obtained immortality at the time of the Great Flood, from which he saved himself and his family and his beasts and his belongings; the account which he gives of these events resembles that given in the Bible.

Utnapishtim then speaks to Gilgamesh of a wonder-working plant, which has the power to restore youth. It lies at the bottom of the sea, and the hero dives down thither and brings back the plant with him. He sets off once more, but during the journey he goes down to a watercourse to wash, and while he is there a serpent is attracted by the scent of the plant, and carries it away. Gilgamesh will not attain immortality.

His fate is sealed. He now conceives the desire to have his dead friend Enkidu come back from the underworld and speak to him of life beyond the grave. The poem comes to a gloomy end with the comfortless picture of that life.

The last of the twelve tablets of this epic, the one in which this meeting with Enkidu is recorded, would seem from Professor Kramer's recent studies to be a later supplement, not belonging to the original poem. Those studies have also shown that the composition has brought together a number of Sumerian themes, and knit them into an ordered whole.

The idea of man's striving after eternal life, and failing through no fault of his own (for we find here no conception corresponding to the Hebrew one of original sin) is treated in a different manner in another poem, recounting the myth of Adapa. Adapa was a fisherman, and a son of the god Ea. One day a gust of the South Wind overturned his boat, and in his anger he seized the wind and broke its wings. When he was summoned before the supreme god Anu to answer for his behaviour, his father Ea, fearing the angry god would seek to poison him, warned him to refuse all offers of food or drink. In fact, however, Anu was so impressed by Adapa's wisdom that he offered him the food and water of life. Mindful of his father's warning, Adapa refused, and so for ever lost immortality.

Another hero who sought to mount to heaven was the legendary king Etana. He was childless and therefore desired the "birth-herb", to get which he set out for heaven on the back of an eagle which he had rescued from a serpent; but his adventurous flight did not attain its goal.

Themes drawn from this literature are common in Mesopotamian art. Thus we have in particular a multitude of representations of the plant or tree of life, in the form of a conventionalized palmtree, which served as the symbol of the everlasting renewal of life.

Mesopotamian lyric is exclusively religious: we have hymns, penitential psalms and prayers, which express in various forms that cult of the gods which was of the very essence of the life of those peoples. Many of these lyrics are composed according to fixed schemes, but are not lacking in true lyrical spirit and human feeling. Their constant themes are the exaltation of the gods, their attributes, their glorious deeds and mercies. The following example is taken from a hymn to the sun-god Shamash:

> "O Shamash, king of heaven and earth,
> Who orderest all things high and low,
> Shamash, the wakening to life of the dead
> And the freeing of the captive is in thy hand.
> Incorruptible judge,
> Who orderest mankind,
> Exalted scion
> Of the Lord Namrassit,

Most mighty and noble son,
Light of the lands,
Maker of all that is in heaven and on the earth,
Shamash, art thou."[1]

Here is a prayer addressed by Sargon II of Assyria to the god Ninigiku (another name of Ea):

"O Ninigiku, lord of wisdom,
Thou who hast formed the universe,
May thy fountains be opened for Sargon, king of the
world, king of Assyria, governor of Babylon, king
of Sumer and Akkad, the builder of thy sanctuary;
May thy fountains bring the water of prosperity and
plenty, and water his land!
Wide experience and broad understanding
Ordain as his lot;
Bring his work to fulfilment,
And let him attain to his goal!"[2]

On the foundations of the earlier Sumerian tradition was built up an extensive didactic and sapiential literature, in alternate prose and verse, rich in counsels and proverbs of remarkable wisdom. Here are some of the counsels, striking for their exalted moral tone:

"Do no ill to thy opponent;
Render good to him who does thee ill;
Act justly with thy foe . . .
Piety engenders well-being,
Sacrifice prolongs life,
Prayer atones for sin."[3]

[1] Cf. A. Falkenstein—W. von Soden, *Sumerische und akkadische Hymnen und Gebete*, Zürich-Stuttgart 1953, p.321.
[2] Ibid., p.279.
[3] For references cf. J. B. Pritchard, *Ancient Near Eastern Texts* . . . , Princeton, ed.2, 1955, p.426.

Some proverbial expressions:

"My cistern is not dried up, and so I do not feel
very thirsty.
"If I had not gone myself, who would have gone at
my side?
"He consecrated the temple before he began it.
"You go and take the enemy's field, the enemy comes
and takes your field.
"Another's ox eats grass, one's own ox lies down in
the pasture."[1]

An old Sumerian theme which reappears among the Babylonians and the Assyrians, and later again among the Hebrews, is that of the sufferings of the righteous. We find it treated in a work which may well be called the Mesopotamian book of Job. Why is the good man tried by suffering?

" I am now come to the borne of life and passed beyond it;
I look about me: evil upon evil!
My affliction grows, justice I cannot find . . .
Yet I thought only of prayer and supplication,
Invocation was my care, sacrifice my rule;
The day of the worship of the gods was my delight,
The day of my goddess's procession was my profit and
my wealth;
The veneration of the king was my joy,
Music for him my pleasure . . ."[2]

The first answer given to the problem of suffering is that man is not in a position to judge of good and evil. The second is an exhortation to hope: at the height of his affliction the sufferer will be succoured by the gods.

[1] Cf. ibid. p.425, I and III.   [2] Cf. ibid. p.434-435.

A large part of Akkadian prose literature is likewise religious in content. Here we have in the first place many ritual texts, describing priestly procedure and sacred ceremonies, in particular the New Year celebration at Babylon. Next there are the incantations and deprecations, whose importance in the struggle against demons we have seen in the chapter on Mesopotamian religion. These texts contain also passages in verse, in the form of hymns and prayers to be recited in the course of the ceremonies. There are two chief classes of deprecatory spells, called respectively *maqlū* and *shurpū*. Both of these words mean "burning", and are to be accounted for by the fact that the spells were accompanied by the magical rite of burning some object. There was also an extensive oracular literature, which set forth, along with the appropriate prayers, the petitions addressed to the gods by princes in order to obtain predictions of future events, especially in connection with military enterprises; and we have also the answers made by the gods to the princes. Similar in scope are the divination-texts, couched in the same style as the laws, that is, in the form of a series of propositions beginning with premises introduced by the word *shumma*, "if", and then setting forth the consequences to be deduced in each case. A special branch of this literature dealt with hepatoscopy ("liver-inspection"), of which we spoke earlier in this chapter.

Historical literature, in the sense of the reasoned exposition and analysis of past events, is lacking; what we have are chronicles, that is, lists of the titles and campaigns of the various kings, and of the main events of various years. Kings put their exploits on record in official inscriptions, but from Hammurapi onwards the inscriptions of the Babylonian kings make scarcely any mention of military campaigns, while setting forth at length the works of peace, such as the digging of canals and the erection of temples; hence to complete our knowledge of the history of these reigns we must have recourse to the contemporary chronicles. This idiosyncrasy of the Babylonian sovereigns corresponds to their conception of kingship, while on the other hand the warlike spirit of the north is equally reflected in the Assyrian inscriptions, which give detailed accounts, sometimes in several successive editions, of the monarchs' military campaigns.

An important section of Akkadian literature is devoted to linguistic questions. The Babylonians and Assyrians have left us sign-catalogues and dictionaries in the full sense of the word. The catalogues list the various cuneiform signs and indicate their values; the dictionaries give the correspondences of the two languages of Mesopotamia, Sumerian and Akkadian. There are also dictionaries of synonyms, in an even broader sense of the term than the modern one.

Finally, we have treatises on astronomy, mathematics, geography, medicine, chemistry, zoology and botany: a body of literature truly impressive for its extent and variety.

LEGAL AND SOCIAL INSTITUTIONS

A constant and typical feature of the habits of thought of the Mesopotamian peoples, and one which left its mark on all forms of their social life, was their juridical outlook. A natural tendency to distinguish and codify lies behind the vast system of jurisprudence which was developed by Babylonian and Assyrian civilization and which served in its turn as one of the chief vehicles for the extension of that civilization to the surrounding world.

The fusion of Sumerian and Semitic elements which is so typical of Mesopotamian culture as a whole is here especially noteworthy; once more it is difficult to separate the elements inherited from the Sumerians from those of Semitic origin, though some traces of nomadic inspiration may be distinguished in certain legal provisions and customs.

The great discovery in the field of Mesopotamian law was that of the Code of Hammurapi, which came to light at the beginning of the present century in the ruins of Susa, whither it had been carried off by an Elamite king after an invasion of Babylon. It is in the form of a large stele bearing on its upper portion a relief of the king standing before his god. Under the relief the inscription begins with an introductory passage in which the king exalts the task which the gods have set him of bringing justice on the earth, defending the poor against the rich, and the righteous against wrongdoers. Next follows the body of laws, and then finally a conclusion in which the king once more exalts his work, and trusts that the oppressed may find in it words of comfort and of justice.

Hammurapi's legislation was for long regarded as a highly original creation, but this judgement has since been modified thanks to the discovery of more ancient bodies of law, namely the Code of Bilalama, sovereign of Eshnunna about two centuries before the time of Hammurapi, contained in two tablets found between 1945 and 1947; the equally ancient code, in Sumerian, of Lipit-Ishtar of the dynasty of Isin, found, in four fragments, in Nippur at the end of the last century, but only recently identified and interpreted; and finally, most ancient of all, also in Sumerian, the laws of Ur-Nammu, founder of the third dynasty of Ur, around 2050 B.C., found in 1952. These new discoveries show that the importance of Hammurapi's legislation lies rather in its having collected and codified what was already traditional, than in the originality of its content. This however does not alter the fact that Hammurapi's Code enjoyed a most widespread diffusion and renown, and influenced all subsequent legislation.

We have also a collection of laws from Assyria, belonging to the time of the Middle Empire; as compared with the laws of Hammurapi the Assyrian ones are marked by a much greater severity and a much lower cultural level. Finally, we have neo-Babylonian laws. There is a notable difference in emphasis between Babylonian and Assyrian law, and between the law of one period and that of another.

In addition to the laws, we have a number of contracts, judicial decisions, reports of trials, accounts and receipts, and fiscal and other documents, which complete our acquaintance with Mesopotamian jurisprudence, and show the complexity and high level of development of the legal system.

Babylonian society is represented in the Code of Hammurapi as consisting of three classes. The members of the highest of these, who were called *awīlum*, were the "patricians", enjoying full liberty and all the rights and privileges of citizenship. The second class is composed of citizens called *mushkēnum*, who may be termed "plebeians"; though free men, they were subject to certain legal restrictions, notably in connection with the transfer of immovable property. The third class is that of the *wardum*, that is, the slaves. Among the Assyrians too there was a division into three classes; the two extremes of this division correspond to those of the Babylonian one, but the exact status of the middle class is not certain.

The three classes differ from one another in legal status. For example, offences against plebeians are punished much less severely than offences against patricians; or rather, they are punished according to a different principle:

"If a patrician has destroyed the eye of another, they shall destroy his eye.

If he has broken the bone of another, they shall break his bone.

If he has destroyed the eye of a plebeian or broken the bone of a plebeian, he shall pay one mina of silver."[1]

Here we see an application, restricted to the patricians, of the law of retaliation, of which more will be said in the section on penal law.

Slaves were naturally rated much lower than free men:

---

[1] Code of Hammurapi, art. 196—198.

"If a patrician has given the marriage-gift for the daughter of a patrician, but another takes her by force, without asking the leave of her father and her mother, and takes away her virginity, this is a capital offence, and he shall die . . .

If a patrician takes away the virginity of the slave-girl of another patrician, he shall pay two thirds of a mina of silver; the slave-girl shall remain her master's property."[1]

Slaves were regarded simply as the chattels of their masters, and the only advantage of their state was the protection given them by their masters for that very reason.

Within the family the father had supreme though not unlimited authority. Marriages were concluded by written contract, without which the union was not valid in law. The Code of Hammurapi is explicit on this point:

"If any man has taken a wife, but has not made with her a written contract, that woman is not his wife."[2]

The marriage was preceded by a gift made by the bridegroom to the parents of the bride, a relic of the ancient custom of buying the bride. This gift served as a guarantee against the breach of the contract by either party (Code of Hammurapi, art. 159, 160).

A second wife was commonly taken if the first was childless. Such second wives were often slaves; though they had not the same rights as free spouses, their condition was fairly satisfactory.

Divorce was permitted, and in certain cases, such as the husband's prolonged absence or refusal to support his wife, came into effect automatically. According to the Code of Hammurapi, childlessness was grounds for divorce, but in that case the woman kept her dowry and the marriage-gift (art. 138). A woman might also divorce her husband, if he neglected her or left her; in such a case she had the right to remarry.

[1] Code of Bilalama, art. 26, 31.   [2] Code of Hammurapi, art. 128.

Adultery and rape were punished with the utmost severity (Code of Hammurapi, art. 129), as also were assaults on close relations.

From the Assyrian laws we learn that in that region, from even before the first millennium, it was the custom for ladies of rank and married women to wear veils, whereas this was forbidden under heavy penalties to slaves and harlots.

The status of women in Mesopotamian society was, in conclusion, relatively satisfactory; at least, along with the increase in the force of law in the new social conditions, great progress had been made from the state of affairs that had obtained in desert life.

Right of inheritance in Babylonia was founded on legal succession. The inheritance was divided among the legitimate or legitimated sons without distinction, whether born of the first wife or of another, whether natural or adoptive. Daughters were excluded from inheriting except in the absence of male heirs, but they retained a certain right of usufruct, which was however for life only; in addition they had the right to a gift on the occasion of their marriage. An heir might be disinherited only for grave reasons, certified by the judge.

Written wills were not in use, but their purpose was to some extent served by contracts of adoption, since adopted sons were thereby legal heirs, while the adoptive father might make the validity of the contract of adoption dependent on the execution of certain conditions.

The notion of property underwent a notable evolution in Mesopotamia, when the few movable goods of the desert-dwellers were succeeded by the possessions of a settled community, comprising both movable property, such as grain, gold and silver, boats and the like, and immovable, such as houses, gardens and fields. Immovable property was registered in the administrative archives; a special status was accorded to such property granted in fee by the state to certain categories of its subjects; these concessions (*ilkum*) carried with them the obligation to military service, and, according to circumstances, a contribution levied on the fruits of the earth.

A great part of the documents that have so far come down to us from Babylonian civilization is made up of contracts, which bear witness to the great development of commercial life which had accompanied that of property-owning, and to the elaborate legal system by which commercial dealings were regulated. We have deeds relating to deposits, to transport, to buying and selling and transfer of property, to loans at interest, to leases, to partnership. The Code of Hammurapi lays down certain prescriptions for contracts, for example in the interesting case of land-leases (art. 60, 64).

The multitude of contracts gives us an insight into the economic life of Mesopotamia. The principal occupation of the people was agriculture. The land was very fertile so long as it was irrigated by an efficient canal-system, hence the work of controlling and distributing the waters to which the valley owed its prosperity and its very life was the first care of king and people alike. The seemingly sterile sand-waste transformed itself as soon as it was watered into a green plain, on which in a very short time there arose the date-palms which were the country's great source of wealth. The principal cereal of Mesopotamia was barley, but wheat and rye were also grown. Wine had been known from Sumerian times. Other plants cultivated were sesame, for its oil, the pomegranate, and the mulberry.

Assyria lent itself less well than Babylonia to the cultivation of cereals. A large amount of its territory, however, was mountain-land, where there grew forests, which were a source of timber for building and for tool-making. Even stone, extremely rare in Babylonia, was less so in Assyria, where many temples and even private houses were built of stone. Babylonia on the other hand had to use brick, and brick-making was its principal manufacture, as is to be seen from the many commercial deeds relating to it.

Though stock-raising was no longer for the Semitic peoples of Mesopotamia what it had been for their ancestors in the desert, it retained its own importance, and reached a considerable development, and its exercise was regulated by law. Dairy-farming ensured the supply of milk, butter and cheese.

The canals were not only the foundation of agricultural prosperity, but also the highways of commerce. Great barges laden with oil and grain and all manner of other wares passed continually along them. The waterways were likewise the bearers of much of the passenger-traffic, and of many of the processions of the gods. The Mesopotamians made great use of "collapsible boats" in the form of large bladders of hide. On the banks of the waterways arose great warehouses and provisioning-centres, and the prosperity even of the cities came from their nearness to the water.

Trade with regions inaccessible by sea or river was carried on by caravaneers. From the mouth of the Persian Gulf they set out across the Arabian peninsula, or followed its coastline, making mainly for Arabia Felix. To the north, in addition to the sources of Tigris and Euphrates, there were other routes into Asia Minor, where there was a large Assyrian commercial colony. Babylonian manufactured goods penetrated to the cities of India, whither traders brought them by sea or through Persia.

This vast and active organization of the economic life of the Mesopotamian valley is all the more impressive when we reflect that it was built up at a time when over a large part of the Mediterranean world there had as yet arisen no comparable form of society.

Of all the forms of Mesopotamian law, the Sumerian was the mildest, and the Assyrian the harshest. The Babylonian Code of Hammurapi occupies a middle place between the two extremes.

The death penalty was laid down for many of the more serious offences: in the first place, for calumny and false witness, but also for theft, robbery, and receiving stolen goods.

The law of retaliation governed legislation referring to the patrician class; only in the case of plebeians or slaves was it mitigated. "An eye for an eye and a tooth for a tooth" is the watchword of the Code of Hammurapi; we have already quoted art. 196—198, which exemplify the application of this law to the patricians and its mitigation for other classes of society.

The most recent discoveries show that the law of retaliation was probably introduced by the Semitic people of the first Babylonian dynasty, or at any rate, that it had no place in previous juridical tradition. Thus the laws of Bilalama speak simply of paying damages, and so do the newly-discovered laws of Ur-Nammu:

"If a man has put out with a weapon the eye . . . of another man, he must pay a mina of silver.

If a man has cut off with an instrument . . . the nose of another man, he must pay two thirds of a mina of silver."[1]

The penal law likewise imposed penalties on professional men when they caused accidental damage in the exercise of their profession. For example, according to the Code of Hammurapi surgeons were punished or rewarded according to the results of their operations, with the usual scale of differences according to the patient's social class (art. 215—220). If this seems to us unreasonable, it is more intelligible that architects were penalized for damage caused by jerry-building (art. 229—232).

Minor penalties were affixed to minor faults, such as negligence or incompetence in tilling the soil.

Assyrian law, as has already been remarked, was more cruel than Babylonian. In addition to the punishments in use in Babylon we here find mutilations of fingers, nose, breasts, ears. The following are examples:

"If a male or female slave receive any stolen article from the

[1] Laws of Ur-Nammu, lines 330—334.

wife of a patrician, they shall cut off the nose and ears of the slave in retribution for the theft, and the patrician shall cut off the ears of his wife . . .

If the wife of a patrician commit a theft in another's house, and its value be greater than five minas of lead, the owner of the stolen goods shall affirm on oath: I did not urge her: rob in my house! If the husband consent to redeem her, he shall give back what was stolen and redeem her, and cut off her ears. If he do not consent, the owner of the stolen goods shall take her and cut off her nose."[1]

As for court procedure, cases were tried in the presence of judges to whom the contending parties applied when they could come to no agreement out of court. The judges, after a preliminary examination of the circumstances, allowed the parties to put their cases. The evidence adduced might be in the form of written documents, declarations of witnesses, affidavits sworn before priests, or the so-called river-ordeal ("judgement of God"), in which the person on trial was plunged into the water: if he floated, he was in the right, if he sank he was in the wrong. After sentence had been pronounced, the judges imposed it on the losing party by obliging him to renounce in writing any further claim. This is a sign of the way in which judiciary law had evolved from its original private form, in which the judge was a referee without power of coercion, whereas now the administration of the law was a public service carried out by magistrates appointed by the king, and their sentence was binding.

Lawsuits might be initiated by patricians or by plebeians, and also by married women, but not by the members of the family subject to paternal authority.

Supreme authority in the Mesopotamian state was vested in the king, who received it directly from the god, whom, according

---

[1] Middle Assyrian Laws, Tablet A, 4 and 5.

to the ancient Sumerian conception, he served as his representative and agent, and the peaceloving builder and consecrator of his temples. The Semitic dynasty of Akkad introduced the deification of the sovereign himself, a practice not infrequent in the ancient Near East (in Egypt, for example); but this custom had died out by the time of Hammurapi, from whose time onwards the Sumerian ideal is once more to be seen in the descriptions of the Babylonian kings. It was otherwise in Assyria, where the king, while remaining the god's representative, had essentially martial attributes.

The religious character of all the forms of social life rendered impossible any clear distinction of political power as such. The king was at the same time supreme head of the priesthood, and in that capacity presided over the most important religious functions. Nevertheless at certain periods there arose conflicts between king and priesthood, to the detriment of the state.

Around the royal authority was grouped a mass of offices and officers, as was the case in nearly all the empires of the ancient Near East. The great royal palace and its vast gardens were the centre of a city within the city, having for its citizens ministers, officials, overseers, workmen, priests, and a great variety of other personnel. All this offers a complete contrast to the simplicity of the primitive nomadic state, where the chief lived among his tribesmen as one of them, without pomp and without machinery of state.

In Assyria outstanding importance was acquired by the prime minister, who was at the head of the civil administration, while the exceptional importance there accorded to military affairs gave a position of pre-eminence also to the commander-in-chief of the armed forces and "minister of war".

Mesopotamian artists have left us numerous pictures showing clearly the nature of military equipment. The soldier's defensive armament consisted of shield and helmet, and his weapons were the lance and the battle-axe; bows and arrows were introduced by the Semites, and were one of the chief causes of their success against the Sumerian phalanx. An important tactical arm was the chariotry; the war-chariots were drawn in more ancient times by a species of donkey, but later by horses, when the latter were imported into Mesopotamia during the second millennium before Christ.

The siege-operations depicted in Mesopotamian reliefs recall those of mediaeval Europe. The attackers used siege-engines and entrenchments, and sought to enter the citadel by mining under its walls, while the defenders used bows and arrows and hurled fire and boiling liquids on assault-parties. Conquest was followed by pillage and devastation, and the nobler or more capable classes of the conquered people were deported in order to prevent the outbreak of an insurrection after the withdrawal of the victorious armies.

A country traversed throughout its length by two great rivers, and having a sea-coast, could not be lacking in ships. Mesopotamian men-of-war had several files of rowers, and the prow was prolonged into a great spur. The soldiers made with their shields a bulwark around the deck. The merchant fleet used ships of various kinds: typically Mesopotamian are the great rafts which the merchants of the north used for the transport of stone. After descending the rivers in this manner and unloading their cargo, they dismantled the rafts as well, and sold both stone and timber, both building materials lacking in the south; then they returned north with the caravans. Army and merchants alike used the collapsible boats of which mention has already been made.

ART

There were in the ancient Near East two principal artistic centres, which arose in the great valley-civilizations, and exerted a direct influence on the artistic production of the surrounding regions. The high level of political and cultural development attained by the Egyptians and the Mesopotamians was inevitably reflected in their art, for in ancient times the art of a nation was influenced even more than it is now by the prosperity and unity of the state.

Though Egyptian art was perhaps superior to Mesopotamian in its intrinsic worth, force of circumstances gave to the latter a greater influence beyond its own borders; in addition to serving as a model for the nations round about, it spread far beyond the limits of the Near East.

As in other departments of Mesopotamian culture, the fusion of Babylonian and Assyrian elements with Sumerian ones was so complete that it is often impossible to determine what elements are properly Semitic. This is the essential reason for the great contrast in this respect between the Akkadians and the other Semitic nations, whose artistic production was ordinarily distinguished neither for quantity nor for originality. Here again, the peoples of Mesopotamia stand in a class apart from the rest of the Semitic peoples, and while not ceasing to form part of the Semitic bloc, have a quite distinct individuality of their own. Here we have also a case in which Semitic movement reversed its direction, for the art of the Akkadians was carried in the wake of their armies to the other heirs of the ancient Semites.

The general impression given by Mesopotamian art is one of monumental solemnity. It aimed not at subjective and spontaneous expression on the part of the individual artist, but at the official celebration of great events and the manifestation of the great ideals of the entire nation. Its predominant themes were for that reason the glorification of their gods, their wars and their victories. The artist did not seek to capture his own personal vision and represent objects as he saw them, but carefully ordered them within the regular framework of the established conventions of style. It might indeed be more proper to say that he was not an artist, in the modern sense of the word, but a craftsman.

There is but little place in an art of such a type for the passions and sentiments and movements of the human soul. The characters it portrays are stiff and serene, and even their features are impersonal and conventional. Dramatic or lyric spirit is absent; the striving after symmetry and rhythm of form has led to the establishment of fixed canons and the use of repetition, as with the seals, on which the scene depicted on one side is faithfully reproduced on the other. Conception has taken the place of perception; perspective is lacking. Each part of the composition, even each member of the human body, is set down in its appointed place within the general scheme, in juxtaposition to the others, without regard for the vision of the scene as a whole.

In such conditions one can hardly speak of artistic evolution in the proper sense: although the passage of time brought changes in taste and choice of subject-matter, we very rarely find any traces of conscious innovation; on the contrary, the artist seems to delight in sinking his personality in the anonymity of tradition.

The conventionalism of Mesopotamian art brought about a wide use of symbolism, whereby some characteristic detail serves as an indication of the entire object. A mountain, for example, is represented by stones set one upon another; water, by a series of wavy lines broken at intervals by little whorls or by drawings of fishes.

The only field in which the artistic canons did not overrule the spontaneous tendency to reproduce reality was the portrayal of animals; and here Mesopotamian art attained to heights of perfection which in many cases have never been surpassed. There exist sculptures in the round and in relief of a powerful and dramatic realism, in which the artist's powers of observation and dexterous reproduction of the forms and movements of animals were entirely untrammelled by convention or formalism.

The solemn and monumental character of Babylonian and Assyrian art corresponds to the extent to which those peoples were transformed by the static civilization of the ancient Near East, so different from the comparative dynamism which their heritage of nomadic independence and enterprise lent to most of the Semitic peoples.

The great buildings of ancient Mesopotamia were impressive not for elegance and grace of line, but for their massive majesty. The building-material was largely brick, for stone was lacking in Babylonia, and to be found only in certain regions of Assyria. Construction in brick was on the other hand highly economical, since the land was rich in clay, and the supply of labour was often assured by the employment of prisoners of war.

From the point of view of the archaeologist, it is most fortunate that the buildings were of brick; had they been of stone, little or nothing would now be left of the great cities of the ancients, for their ruins would have served as quarries of building-material for the peoples who came after them. Moreover, when a brick building falls into ruin, the upper portion collapses first and forms a protective covering around the lower portion, which is so preserved for a long time comparatively intact.

The monuments of Mesopotamian architecture are fortresses, palaces and temples. They are built, but on a larger scale, on much the same plan as the private houses, that is to say in the form of a series of rooms grouped round one or more courtyards. A good example of this plan is furnished by the palace at Mari.

The walls were built of layers of bricks joined by clay mortar into a solid and consistent mass impervious to water. They were without windows, which would have weakened their structure, and so they presented a compact mass of surface, broken by ornamental depressions, which in the sunlight created an agreeable pattern of light and shade. Little turrets incorporated into the structure at regular intervals lent it a certain rhythm.

The only real break in the monotony of the outer walls was however that of the rich and elaborate central gateway, surmounted by a vaulted construction and often flanked by guardian-statues representing great human-headed lions or bulls.

The buildings consisted for the most part of one storey only, but had flat terraced roofs, on which the inhabitants could sit or walk in the open air. Domed or cone-shaped roofs also existed, with an opening at the summit to allow the entrance of light and air.

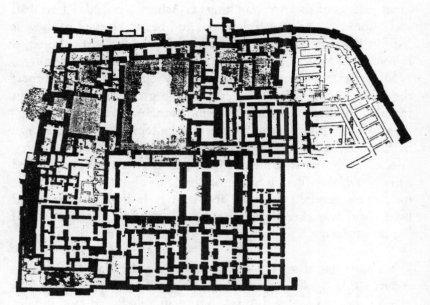

1. Plan of the palace at Mari.

Columns were not unknown in Mesopotamia, but the column as a constructional element would have had to be of stone. The scarcity of stone led however to its being mainly reserved for ornamental purposes, a use which robbed it of its principal advantage. It is the absence of columns as functional elements that gives to Mesopotamian architecture its massive and heavy appearance, especially in Babylonia. In Assyria the greater avail-ability of stone allowed the construction of palace forecourts in the form of colonnades (*bīt khilāni*).

The inner surface of the wall was often faced with alabaster and ornamented with fine reliefs; the space not so covered was often adorned by the use of bricks of various colours built into a pattern. Other walls were covered with paintings or frescos.

The most monumental examples of all these features are the great palaces of the Assyrian kings at Ashur, Nimrud, Khorsabad and Nineveh. The most celebrated and best-preserved of these is Sargon II's palace at Khorsabad. In Babylon the edifices erected by Nebuchadnezzar brought the city to the peak of splendour.

Mesopotamian temples were from ancient times of two types: the "low temple", built directly on the ground, and the "high temple", built on a terrace as foundation. A particular development of the "high temple" is seen in the temple-tower (*ziqqurat*) in the form of a terraced pyramid with about three to seven "decks". The most famous *ziqqurat* is that of Babylon, called *Etemenanki*. Another, which goes back to about 3000 B.C., has now been brought to light at Mari; it is built of sun-baked brick, and was therefore given by the excavators the name of "le massif rouge".

Statuary was not very common among the Babylonians and Assyrians. It would seem that the artists of those peoples, gladly as they portrayed the human figure in relief, did not usually venture to attempt its full-size representation. When they did, their subjects were almost exclusively royal or divine figures, represented in set poses, without expression, stiff and impersonal in their solemnity. Even physical traits are conventionalized, and often the person represented can be identified only by some symbol or by the inscription. The body is motionless, with the arms hanging at the sides, or crossed before the breast in an attitude of devotion. A typical example of this kind of sculpture from more ancient times is the statue of the overseer Ebih-il, found at Mari; an example from more recent times is that of the Assyrian king Ashurnasirpal II, from Nimrud.

In contrast with the human figures, the great lions, bulls and fantastic animals which guarded the gates of temples and palaces show a high degree of realism. The figures are slender and full of power, and show what a high level might have been attained by Mesopotamian art as a whole, had it not been paralysed by stylistic and formalistic prescriptions.

The main part in Mesopotamian sculpture is played by the bas-reliefs. These attain a very high degree of artistry, with their refinement, accuracy and elegance of design, and their almost modern sense of artistic self-expression. The world has rarely known reliefs comparable with those created thousands of years ago by Mesopotamian artists.

The finest ancient Akkadian relief that we have is the stele of Naram-Sin, going back to the twenty-third century before Christ. It celebrates a military victory of that king. The scene depicted is that of a mountain, up which is climbing Naram-Sin, an agile and yet majestic figure, bearing bow and arrows, and wearing a helmet with a horned crest, the emblem of his kingship. In front of him, on a smaller scale to symbolize their abasement, are two of his foes, one bent to the earth with his throat transfixed by a lance, the other joining his hands before him in supplication. Behind the king mount his warriors, bearing long spears with banners. Their bodies are supple and give an impression of motion. Here and there on the mountain trees are to be seen. Neither the figure of the king, nor the others, show any trace of the usual stiffness of Mesopotamian art; on the contrary, the whole design draws the attention irresistibly upwards, and the entire scene is dominated by a lively realism which makes a welcome break in the series of stylized Mesopotamian representations of the human figure.

The famous Code of Hammurapi is engraved on a stele which is surmounted by a relief showing the king standing in homage before the god. The king is bearded and wears a turban; the god has a beard of venerable length and wears a tiara with five pairs of horns; from his shoulders issue two tridents of fire; in one hand he holds the sceptre. This scene served as model for many other Mesopotamian reliefs.

The greatest perfection in sculpture in the round or in relief was attained by Assyrian artists. Some of the rooms of the royal palaces of Assyria bear on their walls series of low reliefs in alabaster or other stone, representing the life and the exploits of the kings. Though the human figures here are still not free from stylistic formalism, the animal scenes have never been surpassed for their vivid realism, in which harmonious composition is united with elegance and accuracy of detail. The most perfect specimens of Assyrian relief that we possess are the hunting-scenes in Ashurbanipal's palace, depicting fish and crabs in the water, running hounds, lion hunts, and the hunting of other wild beasts. The pain of the dying lion, and the terror of the beasts as the hunter bears down on them, are portrayed with a liveliness of expression that has never been surpassed. There is another scene, set in the reedlands, and showing birds flying to and fro in the air, and wild boars on the ground, which impresses itself indelibly upon the memory. The greatest merit of the Ashurbanipal reliefs is their extraordinary freshness and individuality, which gives to each animal a look and a life of its own, and a vivacity which is reflected and embodied in the whole composition. The author of these works was certainly a great artist in the most human and complete sense of the word, whose personality lifted him above the limitations of his environment.

Profane themes, such as those of the reliefs just referred to, are abundant, indeed prevalent, in Assyrian art, and lend it a rougher and more warlike character fully corresponding to the mentality of the Assyrian people.

We have only a few fragments from which to judge Mesopotamian painting; the rest has naturally perished. It is supposed that in general its themes, like its function, must have been analogous to those of the reliefs. Ornamental designs and figures of men and animals were painted in lively colours. White, red, black, blue, green and yellow pigments are known to have been used. The finest wall-paintings which have been recovered up to now are those of Mari, representing a religious procession, several fragments of which have been preserved. The principal scene seems to depict the investiture of the king at the hands of the goddess Ishtar, in a fantastic setting of winged animals and of goddesses bearing flowing vases, a symbol of fertility.

Among the minor arts, that of the potter was practised from prehistoric times, and its evolution serves as a measure of time. Glazed ware is found, and decoration in the form of geometrical designs or animal figures. The most celebrated specimens of the Mesopotamian metal-workers' art are the great reliefs in bronze on the gates of the city of Balawat, representing the exploits of the Assyrian king Shalmaneser III; bronze statuettes are also extant. Ivory-carving is well represented, portraying human and animal figures; so for example at Nimrud, where Mallowan's excavations have brought to light some magnificent specimens: one of these is a fine study of a woman's face, bearing a gentle smile, which has earned it the name "Mona Lisa"; and another represents a negro struggling with a lion in a field of lotus-blossoms. Finally, there is jewellery of very fine workmanship, in no way inferior to that of modern craftsmen.

Mesopotamian seal-making deserves a special mention. The Orientals in general made great use of seals, which served as personal identification-marks. Especially in Mesopotamia, where the type of writing did not leave much room for individually distinctive handwriting, it was customary to sign documents with seals. The prevailing form of seal was the cylinder, on the curved surface of which were engraved the scene and the inscription; a flat impression was then obtained by rolling the cylinder over the surface of the clay. A hole was bored along the axis of the cylinder, which could so be threaded on a cord and worn suspended from the neck. The scenes depicted were mainly of religious character, and the inscriptions recorded the name of the possessor and a dedication to the deity. Especially common were themes which seem to have been drawn from the Gilga-mesh-myth, in particular his struggle with the monster; other common subjects were banquet-scenes and the adoration of the sacred tree.

The art of seal-making was on the whole a variant of that of relief-carving, whose dominant themes and artistic qualities it reproduces in miniature.

CHAPTER FIVE

THE CANAANITES

THE region composed of Palestine and Phoenicia is called in the Bible Canaan, and its inhabitants are called Canaanites. Hence the accepted usage whereby the Semitic predecessors and neighbours of Israel, with the exception of the Aramaeans, who established themselves in the Syrian hinterland, are called Canaanites.

It must be admitted that this terminology is in many respects an unsatisfactory one. Examination of the sources seems to show that the names Canaan and Canaanite meant in the first place Phoenicia and Phoenician, and were only later extended to cover a much wider geographical and ethnical denotation. Nor are the limits of that denotation satisfactorily defined; though they are sufficiently clear after the coming of the Aramaic tribes, this was a comparative late occurrence, and for an earlier period the terms Canaan and Canaanite are applied to the entire Syro-palestinian region and its inhabitants. Finally, Canaanite as a linguistic group is not a true unity; as Professor Friedrich has well remarked, one calls Canaanite any Syropalestinian linguistic element which is not Aramaic; and this negativeness of connotation corresponds to what we have just said of the ethnical sense of the word.

It is undoubtedly desirable that in future the history of Syria and Palestine, or, to use an apt terminology adopted by geographers, of "Syria" in the broad sense, should be treated as one subject, without artificial distinctions. This does not mean that that history forms a simple unity, for this is far from being the case; but it means that either one treats the history of the individual

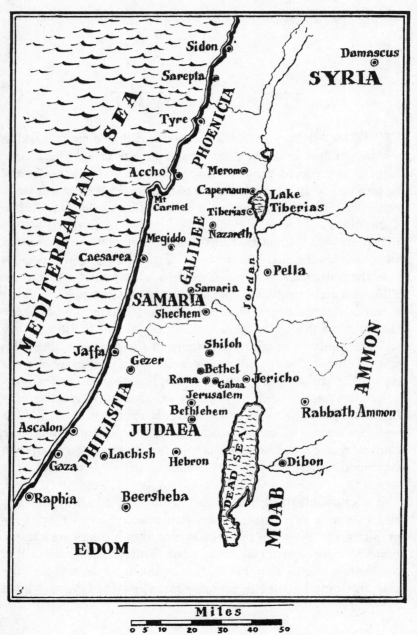

Miles

0 5 10 20 30 40 50

3. Palestine.

elements, and in this case there is no need for terms like "Canaan-ite", since one deals with the Phoenicians and the Moabites and the Edomites and the Ammonites and so on; or one treats the history of the region as a whole, and in this case it is "Syrians" in the broad sense of the word that must be taken into account, in their undeniable individuality between the great peoples on either side of them, and there is no point in the distinction be-tween one element, the Aramaeans, and all the rest lumped together as Canaanites.

Meanwhile we need not abandon the use of that term here, but it must be understood that it is but a conventional heading, under which we propose to describe the political and cultural history of the Semitic peoples of Syria and Palestine, reserving however for fuller treatment in later chapters the two most important elements, namely the Hebrews and the Ara-maeans.

SOURCES

The direct sources of our knowledge of the Canaanites are in the first place the inscriptions found in the Syropalestinian area. The most ancient of these are probably the Sinaitic ones, which may be attributed to the first half of the second millen-nium before Christ. These are obscure, however, and the earliest texts on whose interpretation we can rely belong to the beginning of the second half of the same millennium, where we have the plentiful documentation of Ugarit. This is important enough to be treated on its own, in the following section. Inscriptions from later periods become more and more frequent, and have come down to us from the Moabites, the Edomites, the Ammon-ites, and especially the Phoenicians, whose economic and com-mercial expansion spread the use of their language far beyond the bounds of the motherland, as is to be seen for example from the inscription found in 1947 at Karatepe in Asia Minor, and even more clearly from those found in the Phoenician Mediterranean colonies, above all at Carthage.

In addition to the written documents we have archaeological finds of considerable importance, though not on a scale comparable to that of the Mesopotamian ones. Here too our knowledge has been both increased and modified by recent discoveries. It was thought in the past, for instance, that Canaanite worship was always conducted in the open air, at the sacrificial pillars; we now see that this view was based on insufficient data, on the fact that no temple in the proper sense happened to have been found, whereas now there have been discovered in several of the principal Canaanite cities, such as Alalakh and Ugarit, buildings certainly used for religious worship.

This brings us once more to Ugarit, the most important of the archaeological discoveries made in Syria and Palestine of recent times, and one which merits exposition here in some detail.

The northern portion of the Syrian coast is broken by a series of indentations which form so many little harbours. Near one of these, called Minet el-Beida ("White Harbour"), almost ten miles to the north of Laodicea, a peasant was ploughing his field in the April of 1928, when the ploughshare struck some solid obstacle below the surface, and when the man looked to see what it was, he found what seemed to be part of a ruined tomb. The Beirut *Service des Antiquités* was informed of the discovery, and one of its officials came and not only verified it, but discovered upon inquiry in the neighbourhood that various objects of archaeological nature had been found in the past in the same region. Excavations were begun at the beginning of 1929, and the researchers were led to the discovery that a hill about half a mile from the shore, between the two branches of a torrent which then united to run down to the sea, covered the remains of an ancient city. The modern Arabic name of the hill was Ras Shamra, that is, "Fennel Head", but the archaeologists soon found that the ruins which it covered were those of Ugarit, an ancient city mentioned in Egyptian, Mesopotamian and Hittite documents. As the excavations went on, there came to light tombs, pottery, statuettes, ornaments, animal bones, and finally tablets with inscriptions in cuneiform characters. So great was the success that an expedition of excavation was organized each succeeding year, under the direction of the French archaeologist Schaeffer; work was broken off in 1939 on account of the war, but was resumed once more in 1950, and is still continuing. What has so far been explored is in fact only a relatively small part of the ancient city.

The texts found at Ras Shamra were in several languages: Akkadian, Egyptian, Hittite, Hurrian, and finally, a hitherto unknown language. Hence there arose the question of the deciphering of this language. It might have been supposed that this task would be as difficult as usual, especially as the script used was unknown; but in fact the problem was solved in a remarkably short time. It was at once noticed that though the tablets and the characters used were Mesopotamian in type, the number of different characters that could be distinguished in the texts was quite small, enough to form not an ideographic sign-list, but an alphabet. Word-division was indicated in the texts, and the words seemed to be for the most part of three or four letters. This suggested that the language might be a Semitic one, and such suppositions as that certain letters were the common Semitic prepositions, or certain words the names of deities, permitted hypothetical values to be assigned to certain characters. Filling in these values and seeking to complete a Semitic text soon led to the desired result.

Ras Shamra has yielded many hundreds of tablets and fragments, and these have revolutionized our knowledge of Canaanite literature, as up to that time Canaanite documents had been extremely scarce. The principal group of texts from Ugarit is that of the epic and mythological poetry, of which the outstanding elements are the tales of Baal and his sister Anat, of Aqhat, and of Keret. The state of preservation of the texts is unfortunately not very good, so that there are many lacunae in their interpretation. Moreover the order of the tablets, and consequently that of the episodes in the epic cycles, is often uncertain.

Other Ugaritic documents are of administrative, diplomatic or religious character. Among the texts in languages other than Ugaritic are to be noted the juridical and political ones in Akkadian: in 1953 the archives of the kings of Ugarit were found, containing their correspondence with the sovereigns of the Hittites and of other states.

These documents must all have been written before the city was destroyed about 1350 B.C. An approximate dating puts them between 1500 and 1400 B.C., but of course in many cases those which we have may be copies or re-editions of more ancient ones.

The texts leave one with the impression that their content does not embody an exclusively Ugaritic tradition, but represents a part of the common stock of Canaanite culture. There is, however, a considerable and complex admixture of elements of foreign origin, from Babylonian to Egyptian, from Hittite to Aegean, and this circumstance reflects the composite and eclectic nature of the culture to which the texts belong. When we add to all this the many and important points of contact linking the Ugaritic texts with the Old Testament, it is easy to understand the great interest aroused by the discoveries, and the extent to which they have occupied the attention of scholars.

Additional information about the Canaanites is to be derived from a series of indirect sources.

The chief of these, which was indeed until a few decades ago almost the only one, is the Old Testament. The Israelites have left us many records of the vicissitudes, and especially of the beliefs, of the peoples among whom they lived and with whom they were in continual contact. The hostile attitude of the Israelite historiographers has not prevented their accounts from being in many points both full and reliable.

Next we have the information to be gathered from the literature and records of the great empires of Mesopotamia and of Egypt, which were continually in contact with the Syropalestinian area which lay between them, and often overran it with their armies. The most important Mesopotamian sources in this respect are the Mari archives for the first half of the second millennium before Christ, which give us many data concerning the states and the rulers both of Mesopotamia and of Upper Syria. For the second half of the same millennium we have the letters found at Tell Amarna in Egypt, and containing the correspondence between the pharaohs Amenophis III and Amenophis IV and Syropalestinian princes.

Other important Egyptian sources are the pharaohs' accounts of their military expeditions in Asia; and even apart from the strictly historical texts there are others which give us information about Palestine and Syria. Thus the so-called "execration-texts" from the beginning of the second millennium before Christ, written on statuettes which were broken for magical purposes, bear the names of Asiatic rulers and states; and tales of travel and adventure, such as the well-known story of Sinuhe, contain interesting impressions of Palestinian and Syrian life as seen through the eyes of the more highly civilized Egyptians.

For Phoenicia there is an originally direct source which has become indirect through its transmission to us at second hand, namely the annals of Tyre, fragments of which are reported by Flavius Josephus. Likewise indirect is the transmission to us of the Phoenician History of Philo of Byblos, a writer who lived about 100 B.C. and wrote in Greek an account of the religious beliefs of his people. His work has come down to us only in quotation in the works of Eusebius of Caesarea and Porphyry. For that matter Philo himself does not claim to be a direct source, since he says he takes his matter from an ancient Phoenician priest named Sanchuniathon. Doubt used to be cast on this assertion, but the texts discovered at Ugarit have amply confirmed the reliability of Philo, whose account is seen to correspond in many points with the direct evidence which they offer us of Phoenician religion, and hence the historical existence of Sanchuniathon has been rendered more probable.

We said earlier that it is in Canaanite sources that the alphabet makes its first appearance; this invention is beyond doubt the greatest contribution which the ancient Syropalestinian peoples have made to civilization.

The invention of the alphabet is the last stage of a long process of evolution, beginning with what does not yet merit the name of writing, namely the use of objects in order to represent or recall to mind certain persons or things or events or ideas. The first writing properly so called is however "pictography", and we have already seen how the Mesopotamian peoples developed such a system, and took the important further step of evolving a phonetic system, in which various signs stand for various syllables. Egyptian hieroglyphic writing developed in a similar manner, and went even further by the use of what is called "acrophony", that is, the restriction of the phonetic value of certain signs to the initial consonant only, thus producing a sort of alphabetic writing; this however remained a mere subordinate auxiliary element in a system of writing predominantly pictographic and syllabic, and retaining the complexity and the ambiguities of such a system.

Our most ancient alphabetic documents come from the Syropalestinian area. The Sinaitic inscriptions which we have already mentioned, to which attention was drawn by Flinders Petrie at the beginning of this century, seem to be alphabetic. They contain signs which show a certain affinity to Egyptian hieroglyphs, but cannot be interpreted as such. Attempts have therefore been made to interpret them as alphabetical signs formed by acrophony in a Semitic language, since it is known that the mines where the inscriptions were found were worked by Semitic miners. The most recent such attempt is that made in 1948 by Professor Albright, who regards the inscriptions as a form of Canaanite alphabetic script. It was formerly held that these inscriptions dated from the beginning of the second millennium before Christ, but Albright puts them on archaeological and historical grounds at around 1500 B.C.

Alphabetic inscriptions have been found also in southern and central Palestine. The most ancient are those found at Gezer, at Lachish and at Shechem, which go back to the seventeenth and sixteenth centuries before Christ, but their interpretation is still matter of discussion. In Phoenicia the most ancient alphabetic documents known to us are those of Ugarit, but these as we have seen are cuneiform in type; the earliest extant alphabetic inscription of Palestinian type is that on the sarcophagus of Ahiram, from the end of the second millennium before Christ. The form of alphabet here used, while directly similar to that of the Palestinian inscriptions, also presents points of more remote similarity to the Sinaitic one.

This completes the picture of the material available for the solution of the important question of the origin of the alphabet. An ancient Greek tradition which was widely believed in the classical world attributes this invention to the Phoenicians. It is certain that it was the Phoenician form of the alphabet that prevailed in the Semitic world, and spread beyond it to give rise to the Greek and Latin alphabets. It is certain also that the alphabet was born in the Syropalestinian area; it is less certain that the original invention is to be ascribed to the Phoenicians in particular, but there are many arguments in favour of such an attribution. Egyptian use of the principle of acrophony may have furnished the inspiration, and the Phoenician ports were the part of Syria and Palestine in closest contact with Egypt. Moreover the most likely explanation of the original models on which the letters were based—supposing that they were based on models—is that which derives them from Egyptian hieroglyphs. A cuneiform origin is less likely, although it is possible that more than one source was drawn upon for models, and we have in Ugarit an alphabet of cuneiform type.

HISTORY

In describing the geographical features of the Syropalestinian coastal region, we mentioned in anticipation its historical destiny, determined as it was by the natural conditions. The concentration within that narrow strip of land of the principal ways of communication between three continents meant that it was fated to be the scene of a series of migrations and invasions, without any lasting possibility of the establishment of strong political organisms. It was a testing-ground for the commercial and military ambitions and rivalries of the great powers between which it lay. Migrating peoples poured into it again and again, for it was a region attractive in itself for its fertility, and one open to access on all sides and offering further passage in all directions; in addition to the desert, from which came the Semitic nomads, it was open to Egypt, to Mesopotamia, to Asia Minor and to the Mediterranean.

Its history, then, is a thoroughly fragmentary one, formed of continual ethnic and political changes bewildering to the observer and resisting the historian's attempts at systematization. It is for all that a most interesting history, if for the fact alone that it gives the background to that of Israel. When the Hebrews conquered Palestine towards the end of the second millennium before Christ, they were not the first Semitic people in that field; others had been there long before them.

We have no information about the first penetration of Semitic peoples into Syria and Palestine. When our historical documentation begins, they seem to be already present there; at any rate, the names of rivers, of mountains and of cities are in great measure Semitic ones.

Politically these most ancient historical inhabitants were organized in city-states, built on elevated ground and fortified; but outside the cities a large part of the population must have remained nomadic, moving from place to place and exerting pressure on the settled centres.

Egyptian sources, confirmed by archaeological data, show us that Egypt enjoyed from the beginnings of history a position of political and economic supremacy over the whole region. This hegemony was from time to time reinforced by military expeditions and the levying of tribute, a fact which at the same time indicates the unsettled conditions prevailing.

At the beginning of the second millennium before Christ the Egyptian "execration-texts" furnish a series of names of Syropalestinian states and rulers. The personal names are of the type proper to the Amorites, the people which at the same period was occupying Mesopotamia. It is therefore a plausible suggestion that they existed as a ruling class over a wide stretch of country from Mesopotamia to Palestine. Politically the Amorites also were organized in little states, and were still satellites of Egypt, except in the extreme north, where such states as Aleppo, Qatna and Carchemish lay within the Mesopotamian sphere of influence.

Attention may here be drawn to the difference between the policies followed in Syria and Palestine by the Egyptians and by the Mesopotamian states. The latter, whenever they are able to do so, endeavour to secure permanent conquests, and do not hesitate to have recourse for that end even to mass-deportations of the conquered population. The Egyptians on the other hand content themselves with imposing tribute on the local princelings, or, at most, with controlling their activities through Egyptian "residents". Their aims were economic rather than political, and hence their methods were much less harsh.

Egyptian dominion underwent a check when Egypt itself was subject to Hyksos rule (about 1670—1570 B.C.). The origin of the Hyksos is still a disputed question; what is certain is that they came from the East, and that there was in them a Semitic strain.

With the end of the Hyksos interlude Egypt recovered the old hegemony, save for the presence in the north of a new rival power: the Hittites, who spread from Anatolia to establish themselves also in northern Syria. Hittite rule was even milder, at least in form, than Egyptian: the little local satellite-states had the status of allies, bound by bilateral treaties, and ostensibly retained their full independence.

For the period which immediately preceded the coming of Israel, that is, for the fourteenth and thirteenth centuries before Christ, we have the extensive documentation furnished by the archives of Tell Amarna and of Ugarit. Egypt was passing through a period of crisis, and the Syropalestinian states—Jerusalem, Gezer, Shechem, Megiddo, Accho, Tyre, Damascus, Sidon, Byblos, and yet others—took advantage of this to increase their own independence. They were in a more or less permanent state of war among themselves, and no one of them succeeded in maintaining a position of predominance. The largest state to establish itself was that of Amurru, in the north, which owed its success to the ability with which it played off against each other the Egyptians and the Hittites.

This state of affairs was not to last for long; about 1200 B.C., after various preliminary skirmishes, the whole of the Near East was attacked by invaders from the sea. These "peoples of the sea" in a series of lightning campaigns destroyed the Hittite empire and forced Egypt to abandon Syria and Palestine. A group of the invaders established itself permanently in Palestine: the Philistines; while the withdrawal of the newcomers from other parts of the Syropalestinian area left a political vacuum which was soon filled by the influx of a number of Semitic peoples. In the south the principal invaders were the Hebrew tribes, but along with them appeared also the Midianites, the Edomites, the Moabites, and the Ammonites; and in the north the Aramaeans became predominant.

So far as we know, the political organization of these new-comers resembled that previously prevailing in the region: small local states. One of these, however, took advantage of the weak-ness of its neighbours and of the great powers to unite under its own rule the whole region. This was the Hebrew kingdom: around 1000 B.C. Syria and Palestine were for the first time in history united under the rule of a local dynasty.

The Phoenician cities remained however mainly independent, and the Hebrews followed towards them a policy of friendly relations. This was due to the peaceful attitude adopted by those cities, which were wholly absorbed in commerce and had no political ambitions. We know that within Phoenicia itself a certain position of supremacy was enjoyed until about 1000 B.C. by Sidon, and after that by Tyre. The most characteristic feature of the commercial activity of the Phoenicians is their foundation of a series of colonies along the coasts of the Mediterranean. Phoenician bases appear, at least from 1000 B.C. onwards, in the Aegean islands and in Cilicia, in Malta, Sicily, Sardinia, North Africa and Spain. The most important of these colonies was Carthage, founded from Tyre towards the end of the ninth century before Christ.

The empire of the Israelite kingdom was but a historical interlude. Towards the end of the tenth century before Christ the great powers once more begin to lay hands upon Syria and Palestine, the Hebrew state splits up into two, and the various smaller states resume their independent existence. Political independence, however, was not to last for long. Assyrian expansion, from the eighth century onwards, brought about the annexation, one after another, of the Syrian states, and in the sixth century the Babylonians continued the process in Palestine. When Babylon fell in 538 to the Persians, the entire region became a province of the Persian empire; and a province it was henceforth to remain, of one empire after another.

RELIGION

The civilization of the Canaanites was determined by their history. The continual passage and interaction of so many peoples brought about a mixed form of culture, made up of many heterogeneous elements. Semitic influence is predominant, thanks to the contribution on the one hand of the Semitic peoples of Syria and Palestine, and on the other, of the Babylonians and Assyrians, whose continual drive to the Mediterranean and towards Egypt brought to Canaan the most typical elements of their civilization.

The other principal influence in Canaanite culture is that of Egypt, which exerted a corresponding pressure in the opposite direction. Relations between Egypt and Canaan, both in the political and in the commercial sphere, were close, constant and extensive, and could not but leave their mark upon Canaanite art, religion and literature. Finally, the non-Semitic peoples who poured into Syria and Palestine from Asia Minor and from the sea brought their own contribution to Canaanite civilization, sometimes, as at Ugarit, bringing about the rise of truly cosmopolitan centres.

Nevertheless, Canaanite social and cultural conditions remained closer to those of the ancient Semitic nomadism than did those of the Babylonians and Assyrians. This was inevitable, for whereas in Mesopotamia the Semites, far from their own bases, inserted themselves into a long and solidly established political and cultural environment with its own individual and uniform character, founded on quite different traditions from their own, in Canaan on the other hand the nomads arriving from the desert were subjected to no such influence from the new environment, and were able to retain more of their own individuality and old traditions. The conditions of their new home, and the manner of their entry into it, did not indeed favour complete passage to settled forms of life, or peaceful assimilation to pre-existing conditions.

On the whole, therefore, Canaanite civilization, less uniform and less original in character than that of Mesopotamia, may be said to be in many points more properly Semitic.

The first thing that strikes one about Canaanite religion is that it is on a much lower cultural plane than that of Mesopotamia; this fact stands out most clearly in the cruelty of some of its rites, and the crudity of the emphasis on sexual elements.

Notable also is the indefinite and fluid character of its pantheon. Canaanite deities not infrequently exchange their attributes and functions and relationships and even their sex, so that it is at times difficult to identify their exact nature and relationship to one another. This circumstance is due in part to the lack of unity among the Canaanites, and in part to the absence of a sufficiently organized priestly class, capable of systematizing religion, as it did in Mesopotamia.

Each city had its own special deities, but these had mostly a place in the general pantheon, and were representative of some function or aspect of the common stock of divinities. This is best exemplified in the Ugarit texts, with their mention of divine personages and events not always directly connected with that city's own worship.

The supreme god of the Canaanites was El. This name is not of itself a proper name, but a Semitic common noun meaning "god". Many peoples used it also, however, as a proper name for the "god" *par excellence*, the supreme god. Like the Babylonian Anu, the Canaanite El remains a fairly remote and obscure figure;

he dwells far from Canaan, "at the source of the two rivers". His appearances in mythology are less frequent than those of certain other deities. His spouse is the goddess Asherah, who is mentioned also in the Bible.

The most outstanding member of the Canaanite pantheon is Baal, who forms the central figure of another divine group. "Baal" also is in its origin a common noun, meaning "master", and so can be applied to various gods. The "Baal" *par excellence*, however, was the god of the storm and the lightning, of rain and the hurricane, corresponding to the Adad of the Babylonians and Aramaeans.

Other Canaanite divine names are derived from the noun *melek*, "king". Among the Ammonites this name appears as that of their national god, in the form Milkom. The god of Tyre takes his name from the same word: Melqart, that is, "king of the city".

Baal is the masculine element of the group of divinities of the vegetation-cycle, which we find also in other Semitic religious traditions. Associated with him in this group are two fertility-goddesses, Anat and Astarte. This latter, mentioned in the Bible as Ashtoreth, or, in the plural, Ashtaroth, is a variant of the Mesopotamian Ishtar, and reproduces to a large extent her characteristics. Both of these goddesses unite, in spite of their apparent incompatibility, the attributes of virginity and motherhood. The forms under which they are represented lay stress on sexual features and symbolism. Anat and Astarte are at the same time the goddesses of war: they are frequently represented in literature and in art as savage and bloodthirsty, delighting in carnage.

The fertility-group is completed by the young god who dies and rises again as does vegetation. This god was worshipped at Byblos under the name Adonis, which is derived from a Semitic word meaning "lord"; and he had the same characteristics as the Babylonian Tammuz.

Among the various natural forces to which divinity was

ascribed in Canaan, the sun and the moon have a remarkably limited place. This is partly to be accounted for by the attribution of solar and lunar characteristics to other deities, but it is certain that the sun and the moon become progressively less important among the Semitic peoples.

Finally, the Canaanites worshipped many divinities taken over from the Egyptians or from the Babylonians; here the composite and eclectic character of their civilization is clearly to be seen. Later identifications and assimilations were to take place between Canaanite and Greek deities.

The religious life of the Canaanites can at present be reconstructed only in a partial and fragmentary fashion. We have a certain amount of direct information in short and partly illegible Ugaritic documents, but our most extensive source is still the indirect evidence of the Old Testament.

The priesthood seems to have attained a fairly considerable development, but not, of course, on a scale of organization comparable to that of the Mesopotamian priesthood. There is mention of high-priests, of sanctuary-guardians, of wailing-women, of sacred prostitutes. Diviners were plentiful enough, and Ugaritic texts bear witness to a number of divination-rites. Finally, we have a special category in the form of the prophets; we lack the necessary data for a full understanding of their place and function in Canaanite religion, but they represent a feature of that religion which has a very interesting counterpart among the Israelites.

Canaanite places of worship were not exclusively, or even principally, in the form of temples; as was to be expected in a more natural and primitive form of religion, outdoor sanctuaries were common, situated near trees or springs or—especially—on hills, the "high places" of which the Bible speaks. The outdoor sanctuary consisted of an enclosure with an altar and, most important, one or more sacred stones, in which the divinity was believed to reside.

In Canaanite sacrifice, along with the usual offerings of animals, human victims are also attested. They were offered, for example, on the occasion of great public calamities, as man's supreme gift to the gods. It is not certain however, though it has often been asserted, that the Canaanites sacrificed children in connection with the erection of buildings; cogent proof of such "foundation-sacrifices" is lacking inasmuch as none of the skeletons found shows any trace of violent death.

Another practice on the same low religious level was that of ritual prostitution. This practice formed part of the fertility-cult which we have already mentioned in connection with the Canaanite gods. It fell into disuse at a later period, thanks to the evolution of Canaanite religion.

The cult of the dead is witnessed to over the whole area by the gifts placed in tombs. This points to a belief in survival after death, but we have no means of determining the exact nature of this belief.

LITERATURE

For us Canaanite literature is mainly restricted to the poems found at Ugarit. As has already been said, there remain many obscurities in their interpretation, and the order in which the tablets are to be taken is not always clear. For the rest, we have some Phoenician traditions which have come down to us in sources of late date, but none the less of considerable value.

Both for its length and for the importance of its subject the most outstanding of the Ugaritic poems is the epic cycle of the god Baal and the goddess Anat. This begins with the tale of the struggle between Baal and the sea-god Yam, ending with the victory of Baal, and then goes on to relate the building of a palace for Baal, and the solemn festivities with which its inauguration was celebrated. The central feature of the cycle is the slaying of Baal, who is brought down to the kingdom of the dead. The ruler of this kingdom is the god Mot; and it is probable that his name means in fact "Death". The disappearance of Baal brings life on earth to a standstill; then the warrior-goddess Anat seeks out Mot and slays him:

> "Maiden Anat draws near to him.
> As the heart of a cow toward her calf,
> As the heart of a ewe toward her lamb,
> So is the heart of Anat for Baal.
> She seizes the god Mot;
> With sword she cleaves him,
> With fan she winnows him,
> With fire she burns him,
> With mill she grinds him,
> In fields she sows him.
> Birds eat the pieces of him,
> Devour the bits of him."[1]

So Baal returns upon earth, and with him fertility and plenty. The myth has no great unity of theme, but is rather a series of episodes connected by the identity of their protagonists. It seems most likely that the story is based for the most part on the cycle of the seasons. Baal is the god of rain and of fertility, who rules upon earth from September to May; Mot is the god of aridity and death, who supplants Baal in summer, only to be driven out once more with the coming of autumn.

Another myth of the gods is the poem of the Dawn and the Sunset. The first part of this sets forth the ritual and the hymns accompanying a religious ceremony in connection with the vintage; the second relates the birth of two deities, whose father is El, and whose names are Dawn and Sunset. The scholar to whom we are especially indebted for the interpretation of this

[1] Text 49. II, 27—37 (ed. Gordon).

117

poem, Professor Gaster, has pointed out that it is in the form of a "libretto" for a seasonal ceremony in dramatic form; and he goes on to maintain that a great part of the mythological poetry both of Ugarit and of the ancient Near East in general originated in this manner, although subsequent redaction may have given it a different form.

The Canaanite creation-myth has come down to us only in the late form in which it is reported by Philo of Byblos. In the beginning, he tells us, was a violent and turbulent wind, and black chaos, from all ages. Then the wind and the chaos united to produce a watery mass which took the shape of an egg. The egg split in two and so there appeared heaven and earth, stars and animals. This story has several points of similarity with the Babylonian and the Biblical accounts of creation.

Of the hero-myths the most outstanding is the Ugaritic Aqhat poem. An ancient king, Daniel, has no son. At last the gods give him a son, Aqhat. The goddess Anat offers Aqhat immortality in exchange for his hunting-bow:

"Ask for life, Aqhat the hero,
Ask for life and I will give it to thee,
For deathlessness and I will grant it to thee.
I will make thee count years with Baal,
With the son of El shalt thou count months.
When Baal gives life, he gives a feast,
Gives a feast for his chosen one and bids him drink,
Makes music and song for him,
Sings a sweet strain;
So will I give life to Aqhat the hero."[1]

But Aqhat answers that he cannot become immortal: here we have the ancient theme of the denial to man of everlasting life.

[1] 2 Aqhat VI, 26—33.

So Anat does not get the bow, and seeks to avenge herself on Aqhat through her minister Yatpan, who kills the youth. Daniel learns of his death through a series of evil omens, and gives himself up to mourning. Aqhat's sister Paghat sets out to avenge him; it seems likely, though the fragmentary state of the text leaves it uncertain, that she slays Yatpan and that Aqhat comes back to life.

A historical basis is probably to be found in another epic, that of Keret. Keret is a king who has lost all his family; the god El appears to him in a dream and bids him conduct a campaign in the land of Udum; he is to conquer its king and marry his daughter, who will give him new progeny. The poem describes the carrying-out of this enterprise. Keret conquers Udum, and when the vanquished king's envoys come to him offering rich presents, he refuses all else and asks for the princess in marriage:

> "Give me the maiden Hurriya,
> The fine-mannered, the first-born,
> Whose grace is as the grace of Anat,
> Whose beauty is as that of Astarte;
> Whose pupils are gems of lapis,
> Whose eyes are alabaster cups.
> El hath granted me her in a dream,
> The father of men in a vision,
> That a scion be born to Keret,
> A child to the servant of El."[1]

The princess becomes Keret's wife and the prophecy is fulfilled. The end of the legend is obscure: Keret falls sick, but seems to be saved by an exorcism.

The poem which we have just described brings us to one of the most interesting of the questions which recent discoveries have raised for orientalists. The theme of a warlike expedition undertaken for the winning or winning back of a fair bride undoubtedly

[1] Keret 289—300.

recalls that of the Iliad; and a number of the characters and situations and expressions of Ugaritic literature suggest contacts with ancient Greek mythology. The question of the relationship between the two literatures is hardly to be answered by making either of them dependent upon the other. What is more likely is that a set of mythological themes spread over the whole Eastern Mediterranean area and influenced the literature of the Near East and of Greece. It is possible that the link between the two regions was the island of Crete; in the case of Keret this may account for the hero's name.

Research into this ancient Mediterranean literary stock is still in its initial stages, and many points remain hypothetical and dubious. There does however seem to be a sound foundation for the view which has just been put forward, especially when the area of investigation is extended to include other similar literatures, Egyptian and Anatolian. It has been pointed out that the theme of the wandering hero, that of the Odyssey, is to be found at an earlier period in Egyptian literature, and that such Greek myths as Hesiod's theogony, or the story of Atlante, are strikingly paralleled in Hittite literature. Finally, the connections between the art of the Near East, of Crete, and of ancient Greece are becoming more and more clear.

It may safely be assumed that these studies will make great progress in the near future, and will show that Greek civilization is organically connected with the literary, religious and historical background which preceded it and was its neighbour; and it may be predicted that one of the results of research will be the close linking-up of ancient Near Eastern and classical culture, and that Canaanite civilization will be of the utmost importance in that research.

ART

Syria and Palestine are far poorer than Mesopotamia in artistic monuments. In Mesopotamia the growth of stable and prosperous empires allowed the development of a flourishing and individual uniform artistic tradition, whereas in Syria and Palestine political division and unrest hampered such a development, and such progress as could be made was repeatedly arrested and undone, and its works destroyed, by the successive waves of invasion and devastation, while at the same time the new elements brought by these invasions gave to the artistic developments a composite and heterogeneous character, in which Mesopotamian, Egyptian, Hittite and Aegean influences alternate or are mingled with one another.

Art in Syria and Palestine is thus characterized by its poverty and by its combinations of alien elements. This was historically inevitable; not only was no durable and united political force able to establish itself in this region, but a large part of it, especially Phoenicia, was not even interested in the establishment of such a force or, consequently, in that of a stable cultural unity; for it was absorbed in commercial ambitions.

There was indeed one branch of architecture which was especially favoured by the historical conditions of Canaan, namely fortress-construction, for the defence of cities against the attacks of the nomads round about them. These constructions had not however any great artistic value; the fortifications which have been found consisted simply of several layers of large rough stone blocks.

Little has remained of Canaanite civil architecture; but the excavations at Ugarit and at Alalakh have furnished examples of royal palaces. These were built on the same plan as the Mesopotamian ones, that is, in the form of one or more courtyards surrounded by rooms; but they are on a much smaller scale.

Religious buildings, as we have already seen, were often mere enclosures in the open air, with an altar and one or more sacred stones. The larger cities, however, had also roofed temples, whose structure, so far as we are able to judge, was closer to the

Mesopotamian model than to that of the other peoples round about.

Canaanite sculpture is lacking in statuary of any considerable size; the few specimens of statues which have come down to us, as for example that of Idrimi recently discovered at Alalakh, are of strikingly crude workmanship. On the other hand, statuettes abound, the predominant type being the nude female figure, with the sexual features deliberately exaggerated, and often with the hands to the breasts; these statuettes represent the fertility-goddess, whose importance we have already seen in dealing with Canaanite religion.

As elsewhere in the ancient Near East, so too in Canaan sculpture in relief was a comparatively flourishing art. There are engraved stelae, such as the well-known one of the god Baal at Ugarit, or one recently discovered in the Israeli excavations at Hazor, which is interesting from the religious point of view in that it bears a design showing two arms raised in prayer, below a solar symbol set within a crescent. The greater part of Canaanite relief-work is however in the form of decoration on small objects. Here our most important material is that from Ugarit; for example, the magnificent dish of embossed gold, bearing a hunting-scene, or the gold cup with engraved bulls, lions and fantastic animals, or the ivory relief of the "goddess of the wild beasts". All these works exhibit to a marked degree the composite nature of Canaanite art in general; for it was here that the fusion of the most diverse influences reached its culmination.

The Phoenicians have left us a large number of stone sarcophagi with a human head modelled on the upper surface. Many such sarcophagi have been found at Sidon.

A few specimens of painting have been found in Phoenician underground burial-chambers, whose walls were decorated in vivid colours, mainly red and green, with designs of flower-garlands and birds, and occasionally also men and animals. Last century Renan saw many such tombs in Syria, but the natives have since destroyed almost all of them, leaving us only scattered traces.

The Canaanites were at their best in the minor arts, where the craftsman's careful workmanship often lent a new grace to the general imitation of foreign models, and freer rein was given to the artist's imagination.

The widespread use of seals led naturally to a great development of the art of making them; and the same is true of jewellery and other ornamental objects, of which there have been found specimens of high artistic value and almost modern appearance. On gold medallions, bracelets and rings we find the favourite designs of palms, heads of lions, wild goats, and birds. Other types of ornament highly valued and much sought after were necklaces, pearls and earrings.

In more recent times the Phoenicians began to coin money. Trade had previously been carried on by means of barter, and it is believed that the practice of cutting ingots of fixed weight and stamping images on them was introduced by Croesus king of Lydia. On the coins of the Phoenician cities, for which Greek ones served as models, we find the symbols of their gods and maritime symbols, as well as animal figures.

Perhaps the most important Phoenician minor art was that of glass-working. It seems probable that this was an Egyptian invention, but the diffusion of various kinds of glass and all manner of glass objects was due to the Phoenician traders; the ready market which they found for such goods led to the development of their manufacture into one of the principal industries and resources of Phoenicia. Phoenician glassware shows very careful craftsmanship and a great variety and vividness of design and colouring.

CHAPTER SIX

THE HEBREWS

A S we have already seen, the invasion of the peoples of the sea and the accompanying decline of the great powers in the second half of the second millennium before Christ gave rise to a relaxation of foreign pressure on the Syropalestinian area, and consequently to the establishment there of stronger and more independent local states than had previously been possible. These states were founded by Semitic peoples who had been present in the area for some time, but who were able to assert themselves only thanks to the favourable circumstances just alluded to. Of these peoples the most important were the Hebrews in Palestine and the Aramaeans in Syria. Naturally, the historical situation which had favoured their self-assertion went on influencing their vicissitudes and their decline, which followed inevitably upon the recovery of the great powers.

The history of the Hebrews and of the Aramaeans is thus from a political point of view an interlude of but modest importance, compared with the history of the great empires of the ancient Near East, and is indeed comparable rather with that of the other Semitic peoples of the same region. The Hebrews and the Aramaeans, however, have other claims to importance. Of the Aramaeans we will speak later; we are here concerned with the singular history of the Hebrew people.

The Hebrews have survived as a nation down to the present day. This survival was not ensured by political power; its cause must be sought, if anywhere, in Hebrew religion, in the tenacious conservation of the ancient faith, which is at the same time the mark of a people apart, since is it founded on the conception of a pact between God and the people of Israel. The conservation of the faith was furthered by that conception, for, seen in its light, the historical misfortunes of the chosen people are but passing manifestations of divine disfavour, merited by the people's sins, and continued faithfulness will bring, in God's good time, a restoration to favour.

So it was that the ancient Hebrew prophets interpreted the vicissitudes of their people, and it was certainly this philosophy of history that gave to the Hebrew people's attachment to their religious and national traditions its unique tenacity. Moreover their religion had in itself a unique vitality, which is witnessed to, apart from its survival in Judaism, by its extension into Christianity and Islam and its conquest, in those forms, of so many millions of mankind. In Christianity and Islam however it passed beyond the stage of being a national religion to become a universal one, while Judaism has retained the specific character of a national religion, and conserved the national consciousness of its faithful, to such an extent indeed, that in our own day, after so long an eclipse, it has even been possible to re-establish Israel as a political power.

HISTORY

Our chief source for the history of the Hebrew people is the Bible, the collection of sacred writings setting forth and interpreting that history. Though the extent and the nature of the information given by the Bible is not uniform throughout, one may say that on the whole Hebrew history is amply documented. For many centuries, until quite recent times, little or nothing, apart from what the Bible tells us, was known of ancient Near Eastern civilization in general, whereas Hebrew history was widely known and formed part of the religious education and culture of the European world.

On the other hand, various problems connected with the sources and the time and manner of composition of the books of the Bible, and especially of the first five books, the Pentateuch, to which we will return later, make the reconstruction of Hebrew history, at least for its early stages, a controversial question.

The account which the Pentateuch gives of Hebrew origins is grouped round three fundamental facts. The first of these is the appearance in Lower Mesopotamia of the primitive Hebrew group: the book of Genesis tells us how Abraham migrated from Ur, going up the Euphrates as far as Haran, and thence coming down into Palestine, and how God promised to him that land. The second is the sojourn in Egypt, ending with oppression at the hands of a pharaoh and the exodus of the Hebrews under the leadership of Moses. The third is the journey from Egypt to Palestine, in the course of which the God of the patriarchs revealed himself to Moses under the name Yahweh, renewed the pact between himself and the seed of Abraham, and promulgated the Law.

This traditional account of the ancient history of the Hebrews finds no direct confirmation in extrabiblical sources, but scholars are now generally agreed that it must have a historical foundation; as to the exact nature of the facts involved, opinions still differ.

Tradition has it that Moses died within sight of the Promised Land, leaving the conquest of that land to his successor Joshua. The Hebrew penetration of Palestine is related in the form of a series of campaigns, directed towards the centre, the north and the south of that region. The mention of Israel on a stele set up by the pharaoh Mer-ne-Ptah, and the archaeological evidence of the destruction of cities, though here there arise certain problems and obscurities, lead to the attribution of these events to the second half of the thirteenth century before Christ.

The Hebrew movement of penetration was not necessarily exclusively one of violent conquest, but may have been carried out in part by a peaceful process of infiltration. The nomadic newcomers assimilated themselves gradually to their new environment, passing from their old manner of life to a settled agricultural one. While they occupied certain cities, they established themselves principally in country regions, which included much hitherto unoccupied territory.

Along with the Canaanites and the non-Semitic groups of inhabitants, it is probable that the newcomers found already established in Palestine, in the central zone, other Hebrew groups, which had not taken part in the Exodus. The fusion between these Hebrews and the newcomers was complete, and soon no trace was left of the distinction between them. With the Canaanites however there took place a process of gradual assimilation which lasted over several centuries; the citadel of Jerusalem was captured only in the time of David.

The ancient Hebrew social system was based on the tribe; the Bible relates the sharing-out among the twelve tribes of the conquered territory. The tribes in their turn were divided into clans analogous to the Roman *gentes*.

The Hebrew tribes were grouped around a central sanctuary situated at Shiloh, a system which has been compared to the Greek amphictyony, being based on a similar principle of religious centralization. The authority of the High Priest was considerable, but it would be an exaggeration to speak of a theocracy, since it was not a political authority. In moments of crisis local chieftains arose as leaders; these were the Judges, who have given their name to a period of Hebrew history which may be put as covering approximately the two centuries which followed the occupation of Palestine. The authority of the Judges was accidental and limited, both in extent and in duration; in this respect it recalls that of the tribal chiefs in the nomadic organization typical of the more ancient phase of Semitic life.

The authority of the Judges was ultimately based on divine favour; in this respect their period has been well called the charismatic age of Israel. The best-known figures of this era include Deborah, the woman who, along with Barak, led six tribes to victory over the Canaanites at Megiddo; Gideon, the conqueror of the Midianites; and Samson, the hero of the struggle against the Philistines.

The conquerors did not have time to consolidate their initial victory in Palestine. The Philistine counter-offensive penetrated from the coastal region further and further inland to the very centre of Israel: Shiloh was destroyed, and the Ark of the Covenant was carried off. Meanwhile Midianites, Moabites, Ammonites and Aramaeans did not cease to harry the outskirts of Israel, and dissension troubled her from within. By the end of the second millennium before Christ, Israel presented a picture of almost complete decadence; from this it was rescued by a reaction in the form of a demand for national unity, which gave rise to the monarchy.

The period of the monarchy was the crucial one in the history of Israel. The example of the peoples surrounding them, and the needs of self-defence, brought about the political union of the Hebrew tribes at a moment when the historical situation was uniquely favourable to the establishment and expansion of their kingdom. On the other hand, that kingdom rested on a precarious foundation, and the policy of centralization and levelling followed by its great kings could not wholly eliminate the disruptive influences within the state.

The strongest of these influences was the rivalry between the northern and the southern tribes, and this was never overcome, but itself overcame the state. Only the choice of such a man as Saul, who belonged to the smallest and most centrally situated of the tribes, allowed in the first place, and then only as a lesser evil, the establishment of the monarchy. Saul's successor David held the kingdom together by a policy of favouring the northern tribes, he himself belonging to the south. Thus he was able to hand on to his successor, Solomon, an undivided kingdom, and it remained undivided during Solomon's prosperous reign; but at

I. Ziqqurat of Nabonidus.

II. Lion from Gate at Nimrud.

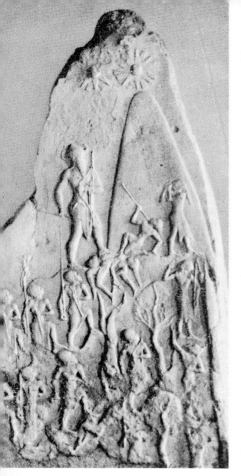

III. Stele of Naram-Sin.

IV. Hunting-scene
from Ashurbanipal's
Palace. (below)

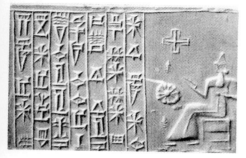

VII. Mesopotamian Seals.

X. Golden Dish
from Ugarit.

XI. "Goddess of the Wild Beasts."

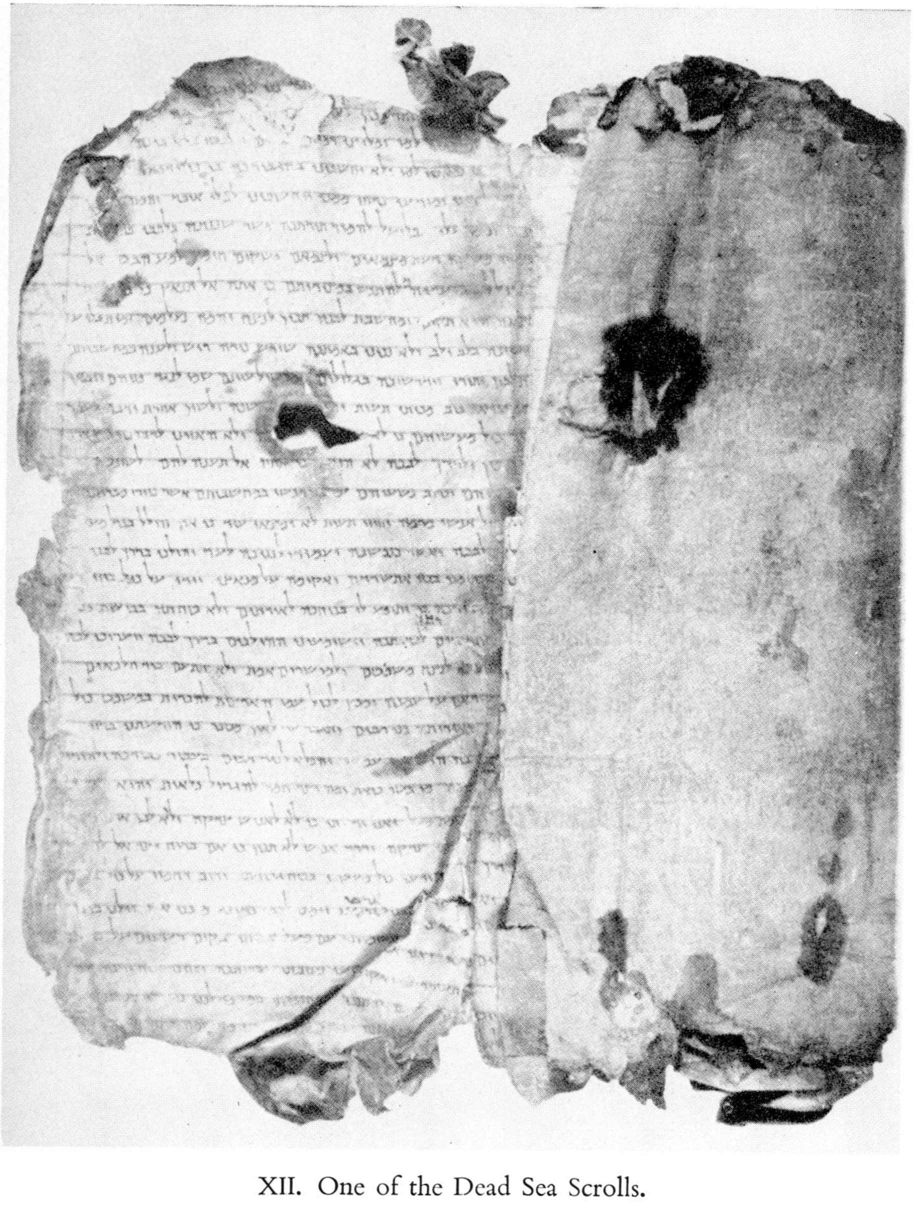

XII. One of the Dead Sea Scrolls.

XIII. Hebrew Seal.

XIV. Ivory Plaque from Samaria.

XV. Relief from Tell Halaf.

XVI. The Fortress of Sam'al.

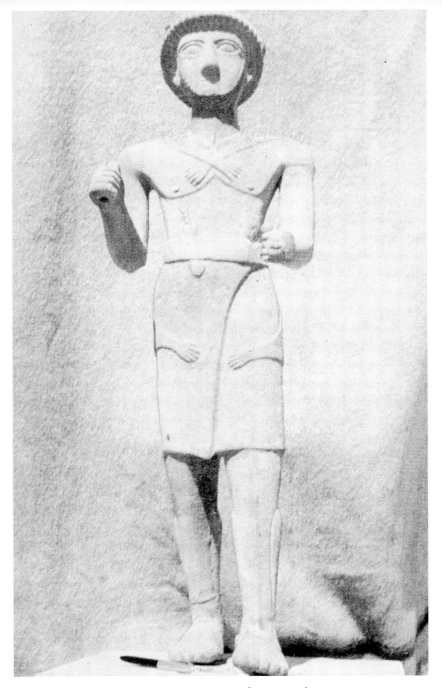

XVII. Bronze Statue from Marib.
(by courtesy of the American Foundation for the Study of Man).

XVIII. South Arabian Bronze Horse.
(by courtesy of the Dumbarton Oaks Collection).

XIX. South Arabian Relief of Camel.

XX. Safaitic Graffito.

XXI. Relief from Palmyra.

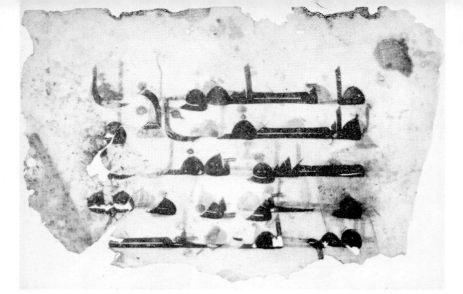

XXII. Fragment of Koranic Manuscript.

XXIII. Obelisk from
Axum.

XXIV. Ethiopic Statue.

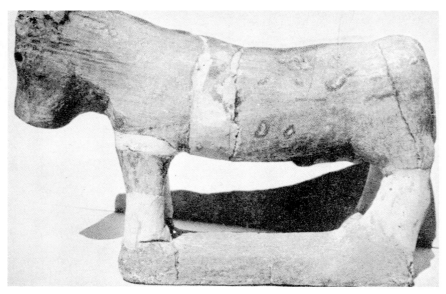

XXV. Alabaster Bull from Haulti.

XXVI. Lioness from Gobedra.

his death the old rivalry reasserted itself and split the kingdom into two.

Even apart from this, the nomad heritage of the Hebrews did not easily adapt itself to monarchy, and while the latter was inevitable if Israel was to take its place in the Eastern political sphere, it was continually hampered and undermined by the democratic and independent spirit of its subjects. Opposition to royal authority found a rallying-point in religious authority, and thus created another dualism within the state, alongside that of the north and the south. Saul soon came into conflict with the priesthood, and this was the ultimate cause of his downfall and the succession of David. David and Solomon, aware of the strength of the "amphictyonic" tradition and of the authority of the high priest, adopted what has always been the policy of kings and emperors in such circumstances: they took religion under their own "protection", attached the High Priest to their court, and strove to make the religious organization a department of the state.

The effect of this policy was likewise that of which history offers us so many other examples: the official, hierarchical priesthood did in fact take on the aspect of state functionaries, and disaffection was now directed against state and official religion alike. So there arose a cleavage between the latter and the religious aspirations of those for whom religion was more than a matter of set formality. Uneasiness grew into opposition, and this opposition expressed itself, after the division of the kingdom, in the prophets. The rise of the prophets was a spontaneous manifestation of popular dissatisfaction with the form which kingly rule had imposed upon religion. The prophets preached fidelity to the ancient conceptions, and were among the first to insist upon that philosophy of history which we have already mentioned as belonging to the essence of Hebrew religion. In the political decline which followed the division of the kingdom they saw the effect of God's displeasure with his unfaithful people.

The history of the undivided monarchy begins with Saul, about 1020 B.C. It may be said of Saul that he was by nature marked out for success in the conditions of the Judges, and failure in those of the monarchy; for he was an imposing and impetuous martial figure with little taste for diplomacy. Hence his sad fate. With admirable success he united almost all the tribes under his leadership against the Philistines, and led them to victory, being rewarded with the kingship; but his inability to control the factions within his kingdom prevented him from consolidating either his victories or his authority, and led to his downfall. Especially fatal to him was his quarrel with his son-in-law David; his breach with the latter brought about the alienation of the powerful priesthood. He went to his death in battle against the Philistines, who were profiting by the disunion of Israel to reconquer the region west of the Jordan and reestablish their hegemony over the Hebrew tribes.

David, who came to the throne about 1000 B.C., restored the fortunes of Israel. He had begun by the formation of a little state in vassalage to the Philistines, and a combination of military and diplomatic ability had won him independence and established him as king of Israel in place of the dynasty of Saul. The capture of Jerusalem and the recovery of the Ark of the Covenant gave to the regenerated state its political and religious centre, and a vigorous and ably conducted policy secured control over Palestine and the surrounding desert areas and a great part of Syria.

Even David's ability was insufficient to keep the peace within the state; at one time, indeed, when his son Absalom put himself at the head of the rebellious, David had to flee for his life beyond the Jordan, and fight his way back to his throne. On the whole, however, his reign was a period of prosperity and wellbeing, which the Jews of later and sadder times idealized into a golden age. Political and commercial life reached a high degree of development, while religion retained to a great extent its primitive simplicity and purity.

David's son Solomon (961—922 B.C.) was very different from his father. He brought about a radical change in the whole life of the kingdom, which he reorganized on the model of the absolute monarchies of the ancient Near East. The pomp and luxury of the court, the great number of wives and concubines demanded by considerations of diplomacy and prestige, and fated, as the Bible puts it, to turn away the heart of the king, and the multiplication of palace-intrigues, represent a system utterly at variance with the traditional Hebrew ways of life and thought, and one whose introduction could not but precipitate a crisis.

Solomon's reign was marked by great commercial development, ensured by the control over the trade-routes of Syria and Palestine, and over that to the Red Sea. Among Solomon's enterprises, many of which were carried out in partnership with the maritime states of Phoenicia, there is recorded an expedition to "Ophir", probably situated on the Somali coast. The books of Kings speak also of horse and chariot trading; this must have been practically a monopoly, since this commerce between Egypt and Syria was one which naturally used the land-routes, and these were entirely in the hands of Israel. The huge royal stables discovered at Megiddo confirm the extent of Solomon's interest in horse-breeding.

Another archaeological discovery throws light on Israel's industrial life: Dr. Glueck has found at Ezion-geber, on the coast of the Red Sea, copper mines and refineries, whose construction shows a remarkably advanced state of knowledge and technique.

There was inevitably another side to this prosperity. The great increase in the size and grandeur of the court, in the extent and complexity of the functions of the state, and in the number and magnitude of the public works undertaken by Solomon forced him to establish a system of taxation which laid upon his people a burden which would have been heavy by any standards, and which weighed all the heavier and was all the more resented, in that taxation of any kind had not entered until recently into their way of life and thought. So heavy was it, indeed, that in spite of all the prosperity the country was heading for an economic crisis, and the economic factor was to play a leading part in the political crisis which in fact followed the death of Solomon.

The most celebrated of Solomon's public enterprises was the erection of the great temple at Jerusalem. In this grandiose project were embodied Phoenician and other Canaanite artistic influences, and also Egyptian and Mesopotamian ones. Hebrew religion itself had not remained exempt from similar influences: tradition reproaches Solomon with the introduction of alien forms of worship; we do not know whether this was more than a diplomatic expedient, but whatever advantages it may have offered from the point of view of foreign policy, it was a step which imperilled the national homogeneity of the Hebrew people.

Hebrew political ascendancy came to an end with the death of Solomon. The old rivalry between the tribes of the north and those of the south broke out in violent form in the revolt of Jeroboam, which led to the splitting of the kingdom into two. The northern kingdom, Israel, was by far the larger and the stronger in military force; but the southern kingdom was less exposed, and had for its capital Jerusalem, the religious centre.

The division of the kingdom was accompanied by religious decadence. To counteract the influence of Jerusalem, Jeroboam restored in the north the ancient sanctuaries of Bethel and Dan; in the south, the kings of Judah remained faithful to the temple, but tolerated the worship of strange gods that had come in under Solomon; and both kingdoms were to see the introduction of pagan worship and practices.

These conditions were responsible for the rise of the prophets. The institution of prophecy is characterized by hostility to the political and religious evolution which had taken place under the monarchy and had resulted in the contamination and corruption of the primitive religion of Yahweh. The prophets inveighed against idolatrous innovations, and were so brought into open opposition to royal authority. It has been acutely observed that prophecy is the expression of the revival of the spirit of freedom inherited from nomadic conditions, and seeing in the monarchy an uncongenial innovation, an importation from the hostile outside world.

Hebrew political history leading up to the exile is set, as it were, to an obbligato accompaniment of prophecy, for the prophets follow all its vicissitudes and bear constant witness against the policy of the rulers. While preaching purity and lowliness of heart, uprightness of conduct, and fidelity to the covenant entered into with God, they interpreted existing and foretold coming misfortunes of the state as brought upon it by the infidelity of its people, led astray by their rulers.

The first great prophets arose in the kingdom of Israel in the ninth century: Elijah and Elisha. To them was due the reaction against the paganism of Ahab, and the abolition of Phoenician forms of worship under Jehu. This reform however did not have lasting results; the old abuses soon made their reappearance, and archaeology gives proof of the frequency of sacred trees of Canaanite type, of altars of incense, of goddess-statuettes and of amulets. A new series of prophets arose in the middle of the eighth century: Amos, Hosea and Micah. Elijah and Elisha had prophesied by action rather than speech, and have left us no prophetic writings, but these new prophets have been called "rhapsodic" ones, because they admonished and exhorted the people by their preaching, which has come down to us in the biblical books which bear their names.

The life of the kingdom of Israel, centred around its capital, Samaria, had been flourishing and prosperous during the reign of Ahab; but already Jehu was forced to humble himself before the Assyrian king Shalmaneser III; and the Aramaeans of Damascus reduced the effective kingdom of his successor Jehoahaz to little more than his capital city. Under Jeroboam II Israel saw its last period of splendour, and then followed the final decline. The Assyrian empire was expanding victoriously towards its acme, and after resisting for a while with varying fortune, the kingdom of Israel finally succumbed with Sargon's capture of Samaria in 722 B.C.

The history of Judah, like that of Israel, was dominated by the rivalry between Egypt and the Mesopotamian states. After a brief period of splendour under Uzziah, the kingdom became tributary to Assyria under Hezekiah, in spite of Jerusalem's deliverance from the besieging forces of Sennacherib about 701 B.C. The persecution of the prophets was at its fiercest under Manasseh, who sought to ingratiate himself with the Assyrians by the introduction of many alien and idolatrous practices. A reaction followed shortly afterwards under Josiah, who carried out a thorough religious reform, with a return to rigid monotheism and the fixing of religious ceremonial. Soon however Judah, caught between Egypt and the rising power of Babylon, was added to the empire of Nebuchadnezzar. Jerusalem twice rebelled, and on the second occasion, in 586 B.C., was taken and ruthlessly destroyed, and the cream of the population was deported to Babylonia. This was the beginning of the Exile.

Two prophetic figures stand out against the stormy background of the history of the kingdom of Judah: those of Isaiah, at the time of the fall of Israel, and of Jeremiah, when in its turn Jerusalem fell. The ruin foretold by Isaiah came to pass under Jeremiah. Both of these prophets extend their denunciation to other nations and to mankind in general, so foreshadowing the insistence which was to be brought above all by the Exile on the conception of the universal rule of Yahweh. The profound pessimism and gloomy resignation of Jeremiah are the last expression of Hebrew throught on the eve of the Exile:

"Thus saith the Lord, Behold I will lay stumbling-blocks before this people: and the fathers and the sons together shall stumble against them; the neighbour and his friend shall perish. Thus saith the Lord, Behold a people cometh from the north country; and a great nation shall be stirred up from the uttermost parts of the earth. They shall lay hold on bow and spear; they are cruel, and have no mercy; their voice roareth like the sea, and they ride upon horses; every one set in array, as a man to the battle, against thee, O daughter of Zion. We have heard the fame thereof; our hands wax feeble: anguish hath taken hold of us, and pangs as of a woman in travail. Go not forth into the field, nor walk by the way; for there is the sword of the enemy, and terror on every side. O daughter of my people, gird thyself with sackcloth, and wallow thyself in ashes: make thee mourning, as for an only son, most bitter lamentation; for the spoiler shall suddenly come upon us."[1]

In their political humiliation, the exiles turned for comfort to their religion, and there took place a profound spiritual renascence. The hope of better things to come expressed itself in the development of the already existing Messianic conception.

This new phase of Hebrew religion finds expression in the visions of Ezekiel, the prophet of the Exile. "Official" religion, and hence the unease and conflict it provoked, had vanished along with the state, and now prophetic tradition joins priestly authority in an intense activity of working out a restatement of the ancient tradition. Monotheistic universalism, freed from the trammels of political particularism, is united with the hope of a renewal of religious life centred around a rebuilt temple.

A great prophet to whom critics have given the name "Second Isaiah" (Deutero-Isaias) because his prophecies have been joined to those of Isaiah, puts forward, along with pure moral monotheism, the concept of suffering as a God-given means of purification. Here, as in the book of Job, Israel attains to that conception of catharsis which marks the end of her ancient history.

[1] Jeremiah 6, 21—26 (the text of the scriptural extracts is that of the English Revised Version).

In 538 B.C. Babylon was conquered by the Persians, and Cyrus allowed the Jews to return from their exile and rebuild the temple. Henceforth, however, except for the brief Maccabean interlude and the nominal rule of the Herods, Palestine is not merely under the hegemony, but under the direct rule of foreign powers; and with the hellenistic and Roman periods it passes outside the limits of strictly Semitic history.

RELIGION

The survival of Hebrew religion throughout the ages lends an especial interest and importance to its study; and although the period with which we are here concerned is but a part of the historical life of Judaism, the fact remains that it is its essentially constitutive period, after which the work of future generations has been one of preservation rather than development.

In the religious as well as in the historical field, the earliest phase here provides matter for controversy. The problem is one of perspective, that is to say, of the assignment to their places, in the process of development of Hebrew religion, of the various elements that go to make up that religion. The Hebrew religious system may be said to be essentially complete, especially as regards ritual, before the foundation of the monarchy. A turning-point in the history of its formation is the entry of the Hebrews into Palestine, with the consequent transition—for all that not a clearcut or complete one—from nomadic pastoral life to settled agricultural life.

The ancient religious heritage sets out from the belief of the people in one God of their own, Yahweh, who promulgated his Law through Moses. The meaning of the name Yahweh is uncertain; in the celebrated passage in Exodus (3, 14) some explain it as meaning "he who is", and others as "he who makes to be", that is, "Creator", and there are still other interpretations. The Hebrew

God is invisible to men, except in particular conditions and under especial forms, and he must not be represented under any form; as the God of a nomad people, he has no fixed abode, but can be everywhere; he has neither family, nor sex; he is holy and just; he has made a special covenant with Israel, and made it his chosen people.

Without temple and without altar, the God of Israel appears amid the clouds and manifests his might in the lightning and the storm. He leads his people in their wanderings, resting on the Ark of the Covenant, a coffer plated with gold and surmounted by the figures of two "cherubim", which the people carried about with them. When at rest, the Ark was kept in a tent—the "tabernacle"—and not until the time of Solomon was a temple substituted for this tent.

A nomad people cannot keep up a constant and regular ritual, but celebrates the great events of pastoral life. The springtime offering of lambs is perhaps the most ancient of these ceremonies, and is linked up by tradition with the Hebrews' exodus from Egypt, and so becomes the Passover; with it is joined the use of unleavened bread, also associated by tradition with the flight from Egypt. Other feasts belong rather to an agricultural setting: shābhū͑ōth, "Weeks", that is, seven weeks after Easter, a feast later called in Greek pentēkostē, "fiftieth", that is, the fiftieth day after Easter—a harvest-feast; sukkōth, "Tents" ("Tabernacles")— a vintage-feast. Very ancient in origin is the use of fasting; the most solemn fast was that of the Atonement (kippūr) on the tenth day of the year.

One day of each week, the Sabbath, was celebrated as a day of rest, and analogously for one year out of seven the earth must lie fallow; that year was called the Sabbatical year, and nothing might be sown or reaped in it. Seven cycles of seven years brought the Jubilee year, on which all land must return to its original possessors.

Circumcision was an ancient Hebrew usage; it was likewise

practiced, however, by other neighbouring peoples, and it is not certain that it was of Semitic origin.

Priestly functions were carried out by the Levites, who probably formed a tribe, to which new members, not belonging to it by birth, might be aggregated. From the earliest times a certain authority was possessed by the seers, professional diviners; at a later time this institution was to have a considerable influence in the rise of the prophets.

The establishment of the Hebrew tribes in Palestine was followed by the adoption of various elements drawn from Canaanite civilization. The book of Judges explicitly condemns departure from the Law of Moses (2, 11—13). At the same time, however, contact with other peoples brought about, by contrast, a consolidation of the people's fidelity to Yahweh, as their own national God; and the events of the period of the Judges were seen as the struggle between Yahweh and the gods of the Canaanites.

With Saul and David, the monarchy saw a noteworthy consolidation of the religion of Yahweh. The transference of the Ark of the Covenant to Jerusalem marked a centralization of the national religion in the national capital. Under David the ideals of the priesthood coincided with those of the king, and for a while, thanks to this harmony, Israel knew religious peace and prosperity. Solomon's policy, however, put an end to this alliance; though he may seem to have rendered to Yahweh the highest possible homage in building the temple, his acceptance of alien forms of worship inevitably created a conflict between political and religious loyalty, and led to political and religious crisis.

The period of the two kingdoms saw the results of this double crisis in the decline of political power, along with the rise of a new religious force, that of the prophets. The prophetic movement came to check and reverse the process of assimilation to Canaanite religion which had been gradually taking place, to recall the faithful to the ancient traditions, and so to ensure the continuity of the religion of Yahweh, and establish it solidly, against the day when it was to become the only force which prevented the complete dissolution of the Hebrew people, who without it would have disappeared for ever.

We have already spoken of the political role of the prophets; it remains here to speak of their religious role. The Hebrew name for "prophet" was *nābhī*; this word has been the object of much discussion, but the most exact interpretation of it would seem to be "one who is called": called, that is, by God. The prophet is chosen and inspired by God to be the bearer of his message to men, and is wholly dedicated to God—hence the prophet was often referred to as "the man of God".

The prophetic vocation was thus founded on a *charisma*, on the grace of God. It came to the prophet, according to the biblical account, spontaneously, often contrary to expectation and desire. It is therefore a compulsive phenomenon. It does not follow, however, from this alone that it is to be contrasted with the priesthood: Professors Johnson and Haldar have brought out the fact that the prophets were often united in associations and formed part of the personnel of the sanctuary.

He who had received the prophetic vocation went into market-place, temple or palace, and preached what he was moved to preach, whether his hearer was the man in the street, the priest or the king. The themes of his preaching followed two main lines: on the one hand he insisted on pure monotheism, rejecting all manner of concession or compromise with alien or idolatrous worship; on the other, he inculcated moral righteousness, inveighing against that licentiousness which was itself ultimately but an outcome of religious laxity. Whether he preached on purity of worship or of conduct, he did not fail to drive home his lesson by foretelling the retribution that would follow if his words were not heeded: this leitmotiv summed up the prophets' outlook on the course of history.

That purity and holiness of life which the prophet inculcated upon others he sought to realize in himself. Not infrequently prophets retired into the desert to live as hermits, or in other manners led lives of ascetical austerity. All their thought was pervaded by a longing after the ancient simplicity of life, that nomadic ideal which remained a living force in so many Semitic peoples. Obviously a phenomenon of so personal a nature as prophecy cannot be adequately explained in terms of an atavistic aspiration; too much original genius went into the making of the thought and work of Amos, of Jeremiah, of Isaiah, and of so many others, for such an explanation to suffice; but it may be said in general that their preaching arose from and appealed to a sentiment typical of the ancient pastoral folk to whom was vouchsafed in the desert a vision of a simpler and grander religious ideal than that which prevailed in the more sophisticated kingdoms.

We have already mentioned the divison of the prophetic movement into two phases of preaching by deed and preaching by word, and we have seen in outline the history of its struggle against religious syncretism and contamination. We must now sketch the development of the fundamental religious conceptions of the prophets.

Elijah's vision on Mount Horeb, described in the first book of Kings (19, 11—13), offers a vivid illustration of the increase in the spirituality of the concept of the divinity. While remaining personal, God is conceived less and less anthropomorphically; his appearances are progressively relegated to the sphere of poetical imagination.

Many religious conceptions more or less clearly outlined in earlier times now assume a more precise definition and formulation, from that of creation and the initial blessed state of mankind and the consequences of man's fall, to the notions of what lies beyond the grave. One conception in particular is brought from time to time into greater prominence by political crisis, and comes clearly to the fore with the fall of the kingdoms: the Messianic one. This is how Isaiah expresses it:

"There shall come forth a shoot out of the stock of Jesse[1], and a branch out of his roots shall bear fruit: and the spirit of the Lord shall rest upon him, the spirit of wisdom and understanding, the spirit of counsel and might, the spirit of knowledge and of the fear of the Lord; and his delight shall be in the fear of the Lord: and he shall not judge after the sight of the eyes, neither reprove after the hearing of his ears: but with righteousness shall he judge the poor, and reprove with equity the meek of the earth: and he shall smite the earth with the rod of his mouth, and with the breath of his lips shall he slay the wicked. And righteousness shall be the girdle of his loins, and faithfulness the girdle of his reins. And the wolf shall dwell with the lamb, and the leopard shall lie down with the kid; and the calf and the young lion and the fatling together; and a little child shall lead them. And the cow and the bear shall feed; their young ones shall lie down together: and the lion shall eat straw like the ox. And the suckling child shall play on the hole of the asp, and the weaned child shall put his hand on the basilisk's den. They shall not hurt nor destroy in all my holy mountain; for the earth shall be full of the knowledge of the Lord, as the waters cover the sea. And it shall come to pass in that day, that the root of Jesse, which standeth for an ensign of the peoples, unto him shall the nations seek; and his resting-place shall be glorious."[2]

The Messianic hope was a longing for the return of the kingdom of David, seen as a golden age and the reversal of present misfortune; it persisted throughout this last phase of Hebrew religious thought, and became the starting-point of the Christian revelation.

In its essence the Messianic outlook is but the perpetual Hebrew reliance upon God's covenant. Through the ages the pact made by God to Abraham is repeated and renewed, and in this, its latest form, it promises, in return for Israel's perseverance and

[1] The father of David.　　　　　　　　[2] Isaiah 11, 1—10.

fidelity in the time of trial which her backsliding has brought upon her, a happy age to come, in which all fear shall be banished, and peace and love shall reign upon earth.

The religious ideals of Israel were in many ways purified and elevated during the Exile. On the one hand, the disappearance of the nation as a distinct political bloc allowed Hebrew thought to realize and affirm more clearly than ever before that Yahweh is the one and only God of the universe and of all mankind. On the other hand, the sufferings of the Exile, and the cessation of the temple-ritual, brought about a return to God and a preoccupation with the inner meaning of religion. The people's misfortunes were interpreted in religious terms, as a purificatory experience, preparing the nation to rise again in worthiness.

Alongside this renascence of religious feeling there took place a development and a consolidation of formulated and codified religion. Representative of this combination of prophetic idealism and priestly legalism is the priest-prophet Ezekiel. As a natural consequence of the conditions of the Exile, the priesthood turned its attention to an organized study of the law, and was thence led to undertake the edition of the sacred books. These traditional sources of Hebrew history and faith were collected and arranged in their three great sections, Law, Prophets, and Writings, for faithful transmission to generations to come.

The return from exile after the victory of Cyrus, and the restoration of the temple, seemed to give grounds for hoping that the aspirations of the exiles were to be realized, and their plans to be put into practice; but they were not to be left in peace. New troubles and crises and restorations succeeded one another, and in fact the history of the Jewish people, as an independent entity, was at an end; the Maccabean revival was but an ephemeral episode. Among the Jews, on the threshold of their new destiny, may be distinguished two outstanding religious tendencies, one of prophetic and the other of priestly character. The former is the more intimate and universal, the latter the more outward and national. Judaism was to develop by means of the interaction of these two forces. While the national spirit was jealously to preserve the ancient forms throughout the centuries, the prophetic vision was to develop into a universalistic movement, which was to be the heritage of Christianity.

THE BIBLE

A prevalence of religious motives over other aspects of culture is, as we have seen, characteristic of the history and civilization of the ancient Near East in general; rarely however has religion absorbed and dominated all other cultural elements, and excluded those uncongenial to itself, to such a degree as with the Hebrews.

One example may be mentioned to illustrate this point. The religious prohibition of any representation of the divinity cut off the possibility of artistic development to such an extent that when Solomon came to build his temple he had to call in foreign artists. Neither painting nor sculpture was able to develop in such conditions; for it is above all from religious themes that they draw their inspiration.

From the most ancient times the chief effort of the Hebrews of succeeding generations was directed to the preservation and transmission to posterity of the tradition in which the national history and faith was contained. The result of their zeal has come down to us in the form of a book, or rather, of a collection of books, constituting the greatest literary achievement of the Hebrew people of ancient times: the Old Testament.

Not all of ancient Hebrew literature has been so preserved. The biblical books themselves refer to the sources from which they drew their matter. Moreover, the Hebrew manuscripts recently discovered near the Dead Sea contain, in addition to biblical texts, other writings, not included in the Old Testament. The essential reason for the preservation, in the Old Testament, of the books which it contains, and of no others, is that the formation of that collection of books had not a literary, but a religious purpose. Those books were chosen which were to serve for religious instruction, which contained religious precepts and religious history; and under this latter heading was included the history of the Jewish people, in so far as it represented that of the covenant between God and Israel.

This outlook upon history, of which we have already spoken, brings it about that the Bible's teaching is exposed rather in what might be called narrative form, than in a systematic arrangement. Legal and moral prescriptions, practical instructions and prophetic preaching have for the most part been set down as they occurred in their historical setting.

The Old Testament opens with the five books of the Pentateuch. The first of these, Genesis, tells of the origin of the universe and of mankind, traces the history of man up to the formation, with Abraham and his family, of the nucleus of the Hebrew people, and relates the migrations of the Hebrew patriarchs in Palestine and finally into Egypt. The second book, Exodus, is dominated by the figure of Moses, and relates the flight from Egypt and, above all, the promulgation of the Law on Sinai. Legal prescriptions, mostly of ritual character, are continued in the next two books, Leviticus and Numbers, which carry on the account of the wanderings in the desert up to the arrival on the eastern bank of the Jordan. The last of the five books, Deuteronomy, sets forth more legal prescriptions in the form of the last dispositions made by Moses, before he dies within sight of the Promised Land.

Such is the form in which the Pentateuch now presents itself; but, just as it is the essential basis of the whole of the Old Testament and of Hebrew religion, so too it presents the most fundamental critical problems. On the date of its composition, the identification and dating of its sources, and the value to be attached to them, depends ultimately the entire interpretation of the earliest political and religious history of the Hebrews; so that it is not surprising that it has been the object of long and involved discussion.

Ancient Hebrew and Christian tradition attributed the composition of the Pentateuch, as it stands, simply to Moses. This would put it at the beginning of the Old Testament in order of composition as well as in the chronological order of its subject-matter; and the other books of the Old Testament were likewise supposed to have been composed in the order in which they were arranged.

Realization of the difficulty of accepting this order of composition led, towards the end of the eighteenth century, to a complete critical examination of the question, and the most thorough formulation of the results of the investigation which followed was that given by the celebrated German scholar, Julius Wellhausen. Without entering into the details of the views of Wellhausen and those who uphold his theory, we may say that they invert the traditional order of composition of the Old Testament books, attributing that of the Pentateuch in particular —or rather, of the Hexateuch, for the book of Joshua is included as forming part of the same bloc of composition—to many centuries after the death of Moses. The differences in the names used to refer to the divinity, the duplication of certain narratives, and the remarkable differences of language and style between different parts of the composition convinced the Critical school that the five books attributed to Moses were in fact the result of a process of compilation from different sources. Four principal ones were identified: (1) the "Yahwist" Codex (J), which was composed about 850 B.C. in the kingdom of Judah, and owes its name to its use of the proper name Yahweh, whereas the name Elohim ("God") alone is used in another source, hence called (2) the "Elohist" Codex (E), composed about 770 B.C. in the northern kingdom; these two were united into one compilation (JE) about 650 B.C.; (3) Deuteronomy (D), composed and promulgated as having been found under king Josiah of Judah in 620 B.C., and furnishing the basis of his religious reform; and finally (4) the "Priestly" Codex (P) of the time of Ezra, combined with the preceding sources towards the end of the fifth century before Christ, the result being, at last, the Pentateuch attributed to Moses.

This theory evidently affected the relationship of all the parts of the Old Testament. The prophetical and historical books must have come into existence, in that order, before the final redaction of the Pentateuch, but without being accepted as Scripture until a later date. The order of composition was thus: prophets, historical books, the Law; but the formation of the canon began with the Law, after which the other books were put, not in the order of composition, but in a systematic order according to their subject-matter.

For many years the Wellhausen theory held the field without serious opposition, but with the advance of knowledge, and especially thanks to new archaeological evidence, it has been subjected to a progressive revision. Comparison of Old Testament matter with Mesopotamian (especially juridical), Ugaritic and other sources seems to show that the Pentateuch, or at least, a great part of the sources from which it was compiled, is more archaic than Wellhausen had supposed. Hence modern biblical criticism, though it has not substituted any comparable system for that of Wellhausen, has modified the latter in many points. In the first place, thanks especially to the work of the Swedish school (Engnell and others), attention has been drawn to the inadequacy of the unaided resources of literary criticism, and to the necessity of taking into account the workings of oral tradition which may often have transmitted accounts for long before they were reduced to writing, and of regarding the resultant composition as made up of different strata as well as compiled from different sources (Bentzen). In the second place, the elements of the system have been modified; thus J has been split into two, the new source so distinguished being called L, that is, the Lay Codex, from the absence in it of priestly notions (Eissfeldt); moreover a common ground (G) has been suggested for J and E (Noth); other divisions of the sources have been suggested, as by von Rad for P; and D and P have been assigned earlier dates. Roman Catholic scholars, while accepting the possibility that the Pentateuch was compiled from different sources and contains later modifications and additions, insist on its essentially Mosaic origin.

The problems which arise in connection with the composition of the other books of the Old Testament are in general less serious, and in particular have less effect on the interpretation of Hebrew history and religion, than those connected with the Pentateuch. The historical books take up the history of the chosen people at the point at which the Pentateuch leaves off, and continue it with varying completeness and continuity until the second century before Christ.

The conquest of Canaan, under Joshua, is narrated in the book which bears his name, and the period in which the conquest was consolidated, with varying fortune, under the occasional leadership of local heroes called Judges, is related in the book of that name. This book contains some very ancient passages, such as Deborah's song of victory:

> "For that the leaders took the lead in Israel,
> For that the people offered themselves willingly,
>   bless ye the Lord.
> Hear, O ye kings; give ear, O ye princes;
> I, even I, will sing unto the Lord;
> I will sing praise of the Lord, the God of Israel.
> Lord, when thou wentest forth out of Seir,
> When thou marchedst out of the field of Edom,
> The earth trembled, the heavens also dropped,

Yea, the clouds dropped water;
The mountains flowed down at the presence of the Lord,
Even yon Sinai at the presence of the Lord, the God
of Israel."[1]

The books of Samuel and of Kings offer us a series of detailed
and precise accounts of the period of the united kingdom, and
especially of the reign of David, and a sketch of the history of the
divided kingdoms, which gives us less information, save in the
passages of especial interest to the compiler, who wrote from a
religious point of view. It is probable that this part of the work is
a compilation made by members of the priestly class, as also the
two books of Chronicles, which give a supplementary and
parallel account of the history of the kingdom of Judah.

The fall of the kingdoms marks the end of the consecutive
history offered by the Bible. For later periods we have sporadic
information in the books of Ezra and Nehemiah, which describe
the salient events of the return from exile, and in the books of
Maccabees (not included in the Jewish canon), which deal with
the last revival of Jewish independence.

Within the framework of this history, the books of Ruth,
Tobit, Esther and Judith narrate particular personal episodes,
which supply interesting pictures of everyday life in the various
periods.

Further knowledge of Hebrew history, and a personal interpretation of it, is given in the prophetical books. The earlier
prophets show us the later history of the two kingdoms, and
foretell their fall as the inevitable consequence of their sinfulness.
In Judah we have seen the towering figures of Isaiah and Jeremiah,
of whom the former constantly opposed the policy of reliance
upon foreign support, while the latter preached surrender to
Babylon, chosen instrument of God for the chastisement of his

[1] Judges 5, 2—5.

erring people. During the Exile Ezekiel instructs and comforts his companions, proclaiming the rebirth of the nation. This he expresses in a celebrated passage of great literary power, in the form of a vision:

"The hand of the Lord was upon me, and he carried me out in the spirit and set me down in the midst of the valley; and it was full of bones; and he caused me to pass by them round about: and behold there were very many in the open valley; and lo, they were very dry. And he said unto me, Son of man, can these bones live? And I answered, O Lord God, thou knowest.

Again he said unto me, Prophesy over these bones, and say unto them, O ye dry bones, hear the word of the Lord! Thus saith the Lord God unto these bones: Behold, I will cause breath to enter into you, and ye shall live. And I will lay sinews upon you, and will bring up flesh upon you, and cover you with skin, and put breath in you, and ye shall live; and ye shall know that I am the Lord. So I prophesied as I was commanded: and as I prophesied, there was a noise, and behold an earthquake, and the bones came together, bone to his bone. And I beheld, and lo, there were sinews upon them, and flesh came up, and skin covered them above; but there was no breath in them.

Then he said unto me, Prophesy unto the wind, prophesy, Son of man, and say to the wind, Thus saith the Lord God: Come from the four winds, O breath, and breathe upon these slain, that they may live. So I prophesied as he commanded me, and the breath came into them, and they lived, and stood up upon their feet, an exceeding great army.

Then he said unto me, Son of man, these bones are the whole house of Israel: behold they say, Our bones are dried up, and our hope is lost; we are clean cut off. Therefore prophesy, and say unto them, Thus saith the Lord God: Behold, I will open your graves, and cause you to come out of your graves, O my people; and I will bring you into the land of Israel. And ye shall know that I am the Lord, when I have opened your graves, and caused you to come out of your graves, O my people. And I will put my spirit in you, and ye shall live, and I will place you in your own land: and ye shall know that I the Lord have spoken it and performed it, saith the Lord."[1]

The intricate visions of Daniel mark the transition to the minor prophets, a series of brief compositions in which various episodes provide the occasion for the admonition of the erring people, the foretelling of chastisement, and the promise of the restoration that is to come.

The rest of the Old Testament consists of songs and of wisdom-literature. These writings are predominantly poetical in character, the poetical form being the usual oriental one, consisting in the parallelism of the successive members.

The greatest of the biblical lyrical books, and one of the greatest works of human poetry, is the collection of psalms. This contains a hundred and fifty songs of varying date, some personal in theme, some collective, expressing the praise of God, and man's appeal to him for succour in the various misfortunes which assail him. Many of the psalms are liturgical in character, and were intended for recitation as prayers.

As an example of the poetry of the psalms we may take the following lament of an exile, at the thought of the temple:

> "As the hart panteth after the water brooks,
> So panteth my soul after thee, O God.
> My soul thirsteth for God, for the living God:
> When shall I come and appear before God?
> My tears have been my meat day and night,
> While they continually say unto me, Where is thy God?
> These things I remember, and pour out my soul within
> me.

[1] Ezekiel 37, 1—14.

How I went with the throng, and led them to the house
of God,
With the voice of joy and praise, a multitude keeping
holyday.
Why art thou cast down, O my soul?
And why art thou disquieted within me?
Hope thou in God: for I shall yet praise him,
Who is the health of my countenance, and my God . . ."[1]

Another remarkable Hebrew poetical work is the book of
Lamentations, an example of a literary type not uncommon in
the ancient Near East. Here is the lamentation over fallen
Jerusalem:

"How doth the city sit solitary, that was full of
people!
How is she become as a widow,
She that was great among the nations, and princess
among the provinces,
How is she become tributary!
She weepeth sore in the night, and her tears are
on her cheeks;
Among all her lovers she hath none to comfort her:
All her friends have dealt treacherously with her,
They are become her enemies.
Judah is gone into captivity because of affliction,
and because of great servitude;
She dwelleth among the heathen, she findeth no rest:
All her persecutors overtook her within the straits.
The ways of Zion do mourn, because none have come
to the solemn assembly,
All her gates are desolate, her priests do sigh:
Her virgins are afflicted, and she herself is in
bitterness.

[1] Psalm 42, 1—5.

Her adversaries are become the head, her enemies
    prosper,
For the Lord hath afflicted her for the multitude
    of her transgressions."[1]

A lyrical composition which seems profane in character, but which received a religious interpretation, was included in the canon: the Song of Songs, whose theme is the love of a young shepherd and shepherdess. The shepherdess sings:

"The voice of my beloved! behold he cometh,
Leaping upon the mountains, skipping upon the hills.
My beloved is like a gazelle,
Or a young hart.
Behold, he standeth behind our wall,
He looketh in at the windows, he showeth himself
    through the lattice.
My beloved spake, and said unto me:
Rise up, my love, my fair one, and come away;
For lo, the winter is past,
The rain is over and gone;
The flowers appear upon the earth,
The time of the pruning is come,
And the voice of the turtle is heard in our land.
The fig tree ripeneth her green figs,
And the vines are in blossom,
They give forth their fragrance:
Arise, my love, my fair one, and come away."[2]

A series of maxims and reflections after the manner of similar productions in the literature of neighbouring peoples is to be found in the books of Proverbs and Ecclesiasticus (Ben Sirach), as also in the book of Wisdom, written in Greek for the Jews of Egypt. Here are some examples:

[1] Lamentations 1, 1—6.   [2] Song of Songs 2, 8—13.

"Better is little with the fear of the Lord,
Than great measure and trouble therewith,
Better is a dinner of herbs where love is,
Than a stalled ox and hatred therewith."

"He who is slow to anger is better than the mighty,
And he that ruleth his spirit than he that taketh
   a city."

"Even a fool, when he holdeth his peace, is counted
   wise:
When he shutteth his lips, he is esteemed as prudent."

"The slothful will not plow by reason of the winter,
Therefore shall he beg in harvest, and have nothing."

"It is better to dwell in a desert land,
Than with a contentious and fretful woman."[1]

The theme of the sufferings of the righteous man, which we have already met with in Mesopotamian literature, is to be found once more in the celebrated book of Job:

"I cry unto thee, and thou dost not answer me,
I stand up, and thou lookest at me.
Thou art turned to be cruel to me,
With the might of thy hand thou persecutest me.
Thou liftest me up to the wind, thou causest me
   to ride upon it,
And thou dissolvest me in the storm.
For I know that thou wilt bring me to death,
And to the house appointed for all living . . .
Did I not weep for him that was in trouble,

[1] Proverbs 15, 16—17; 16, 32; 17, 28; 20, 4; 21, 19.

Was not my soul grieved for the needy?
When I looked for good, then evil came,
And when I waited for light, there came darkness."[1]

The first answer to the problem of suffering is here, as also in
the Mesopotamian poem, that man is not in a position to judge.
The second is the vision of the purifying value of suffering,
expressed much more clearly than in the Mesopotamian poem,
thanks to a different conception of the divinity, who in Israel is
known to be supremely just: Job, purified by his sufferings, will
be restored to his erstwhile prosperity.

The wisdom-literature is closed by the poem of the "Preacher"
(Ecclesiastes) on the vanity of all things, and the pointlessness of
the endless round of mundane affairs. This is a late composition,
and shows Greek influence; indeed it might seem closer to Greek
than to Hebrew ways of thinking:

"Vanity and vanities, saith the Preacher;
Vanity of vanities, all is vanity.
What profit hath man of all his labour,
Wherein he laboureth under the sun?
One generation goeth, and another generation cometh,
And the earth abideth for ever.
The sun also ariseth and the sun goeth down,
And hasteth to his place where he ariseth.
The wind goeth toward the south, and turneth about
    unto the north;
It turneth about continually in its course,
And the wind returneth again to its circuits.
All the rivers run into the sea,
Yet the sea is not full;
Unto the place whither the rivers go,
Thither they go again.

[1] Job 30, 20—26.

All things are full of weariness;
Man cannot utter it;
The eye is not satisfied with seeing,
Nor the ear filled with hearing.
That which has been is that which shall be;
And that which hath been done is that which shall be
    done:
And there is no new thing under the sun."[1]

LEGAL AND SOCIAL INSTITUTIONS

According to Hebrew conceptions, civil as well as religious law was derived directly from divine revelation; the civil provisions of the Law and the religious ones did not even fall into different mental categories. Religious life, moral life, legal life were all one, for all prescriptions of whatever kind derived their binding power from God alone, and all cooperated to the same end: ritual exactitude, moral righteousness and the observance of civil law all constituted holiness before the Lord.

A similar outlook was, as we have seen, present throughout the ancient Near East, but among the Hebrews it took on a more accentuated form, for the primitive absence of any political authority, and the acceptance of the authority whether of a Judge or of a king only as that of one raised up by God, or of the "Lord's anointed", gave to even civil law a more properly religious and theocratic aspect.

Although Hebrew civil law was systematic in the sense that it formed an organic part of an integral system for the ruling of the citizen's life, it was, like other legal systems of the ancient Near East, not codified on a systematic plan. Its various provisions are remarkably fragmentary in character, and seem to be a collection of particular decisions, without any clearly discernible ruling principles.

[1] Ecclesiastes 1, 2—9.

In their content, Hebrew laws follow the common tradition of the ancient Near East; they show affinities with Babylonian, Assyrian and Hittite laws, and in particular with the celebrated Code of Hammurapi. On the other hand, Hebrew law had beyond a doubt its own independent development, essentially bound up with the conditions of Hebrew life, which were very different from those of Mesopotamia. Whereas the latter were those of a settled form of life, in a highly-developed state, the Hebrews were still in half-nomadic conditions, between pastoral and agricultural life. In such conditions the law of property was less developed, commercial relations were more primitive, family organization was more patriarchal. In general the tribe loomed larger in the life of the community, and the resulting situation was much closer than the Mesopotamian to the ancient Semitic conditions.

With these social peculiarities we find associated, in Hebrew law, a peculiar moral tinge, which is the outcome of the penetration throughout of religious considerations. Notable, for instance, are such provisions as that of the Jubilee, whereby after each period of fifty years all land returned to its original proprietors; this reflects the religious conception whereby the earth is God's and men are but its tenants for a while. A similar moral purpose is to be discerned in the provisions protecting strangers and widows, orphans and the poor:

"A stranger shalt thou not wrong, neither shalt thou oppress him: for ye were strangers in the land of Egypt. Ye shall not afflict any widow, or fatherless child. If thou afflict them in any wise, and they cry at all unto me, I will surely hear their cry; and my wrath shall wax hot, and I will kill you with the sword; and your wives shall be widows, and your children fatherless.

If thou lend money to any of my people with thee that is poor, thou shalt not be to him as a creditor: neither shalt thou lay upon him usury. If thou at all take thy neighbour's garment to pledge, thou shalt restore it unto him by that the sun goeth down: for that is his only covering, it is the garment for his skin: wherein shall he sleep? and it shall come to pass, when he crieth unto me, that I will hear; for I am gracious."[1]

The provisions of Hebrew law are set forth in various parts of the Pentateuch. Here we have in the first place the ethical-religious laws of Exodus 21, 1 to 23, 19 (the "Book of the Covenant"). These are extended and supplemented, with a particular development of their moral aspect, in chapters 12 to 26 of Deuteronomy. Another group of laws, of mainly religious character, is that of the "Priestly Code", contained chiefly in Leviticus and partly in Exodus and Numbers. Within Leviticus can be distinguished a special collection of laws, the "Holiness Code" (chapters 17 to 26).

Recent studies are emphasizing the fact that a long oral tradition often preceded the written formulation of the laws. This must have been the case with the most celebrated group of Jewish laws, the Ten Commandments, which is found in two redactions, in Exodus 20, 1—17 and in Deuteronomy 5, 6—21, and certainly goes back to a very remote antiquity.

The distinction between patricians and plebeians, typical of Mesopotamian society, corresponded to social conditions much more highly developed than those of the Hebrews, among whom practically no distinction existed between free citizens, who all enjoyed the same rights after attaining their majority, which was fixed in the book of Numbers (1, 3) at twenty years, and served also as the lowest age for military service.

In addition to the free citizens there were the slaves, whether foreign or Israelite. The majority were foreign, and for the most part prisoners of war, though slaves might also be bought: the slave trade was carried on especially by the Phoenicians.

[1] Exodus 22, 21—26.

In the ancient Near East, as we have seen, the slave was regarded as a mere chattel of his master's. This conception is partly reflected in Hebrew law, which fixes, for example, the damages to be paid for the killing of another's slave, and does not punish the master who beats his slave so violently as to cause his death some days later. On the other hand, there are not lacking signs of a more humane conception, and in certain points the law protects the slave against his master. Thus the master who puts out an eye or a tooth of his slave is obliged to set him free (Exodus 21, 26—27); the Sabbath is a day of rest for slaves as well as for free men; runaway slaves must be harboured and protected, and not restored to their masters (Deuteronomy 23, 15—16).

The condition of Israelite slaves was naturally better than that of foreign ones; they had the prerogative of regaining their liberty after seven years of service. Israelites might be enslaved to their creditors for non-payment of debts, and fathers of families had the right, in case of need, to sell their children into slavery.

In addition to the slaves there was another social class which did not enjoy the same rights as the free citizens, namely the foreigners. The Hebrews divided foreigners into two classes: those who were linked with the Hebrew tribes, and had some claim to their protection, and those who had no such claim. The former were of course a comparatively favoured class, but did not enjoy that equality of rights which was accorded in Mesopotamian law.

The uncircumcised were excluded from participation in the Passover rites, and from intermarriage with Hebrews. Hebrews moreover could not become, in the full sense, slaves of foreign masters: they had to be ransomed at the earliest opportunity, and in the mean time must be treated as paid servants.

To an even greater degree, if possible, than was the case in the ancient nomadic society, the real nucleus of Hebrew social life was the family. As was usual, the father's authority was here supreme. Polygamy was legalized, and betrothal took place in the usual Semitic manner, of which we have already spoken: the bridegroom pays the marriage-price and so obtains authority over the bride. Formal contracts are attested but do not seem to have been necessary for the validity of the marriage.

Marriage within certain degrees of kindred was prohibited by a series of provisions, while others forbade marriage with aliens. Deuteronomy's particular insistence on this latter point shows its preoccupation with the danger of assimilation to other peoples. This prohibition, however, fell into desuetude in the course of time, or at least was not rigorously observed in practice, for Hebrew history is full of mixed marriages. After the return from the Exile, Ezra had a hard struggle to obtain the dismissal of the people's alien wives.

A notable matrimonial law was that of the levirate, according to which the widow of a man who dies childless was obliged to marry her late husband's brother.

Divorce, which in the more highly-evolved Mesopotamian society was in certain cases the wife's prerogative, remains in Hebrew law exclusively that of the husband. He can divorce his wife by simply pronouncing the formula: "This woman is not my wife, and I am not her husband"; the custom also existed of drawing up a letter of dismissal. The book of Deuteronomy, however, sets certain limits to the right of divorce, with the evident intention of safeguarding and strengthening the institution of marriage: a man who unjustly accused his bride of not being a virgin was not only obliged to pay a fine, but also precluded from ever divorcing her; similarly, the man who violated an unbetrothed virgin was obliged to marry her and could never divorce her. Adulterers were condemned to death by stoning, along with the woman, if she had consented.

Notwithstanding the nomadic inspiration of ancient Hebrew social institutions, the status of woman was not so inferior as it might seem to have been. Though the wife belonged to her husband, a woman was held in considerable honour, especially as a mother; the commandment to "honour thy father and thy mother" makes no distinction between the two parents.

On the ancient right of inheritance in the Hebrew family we have but scanty fragments of information; we know however that the inheritance was divided among the sons, and that the firstborn had a double share (Deuteronomy 21, 17).

Sons of concubines also must have had a right to inherit, as is shown indirectly by the episode in which Sarah induces Abraham to drive away his concubine Hagar and her son Ishmael, in order that Isaac may not have to share his inheritance with the latter (Genesis 21, 10). There is however no indication of the extent of such a right.

The position of women with regard to inheritance was a very precarious one. A man's wife inherited nothing from him, indeed there are even indications which seem to show that at one time she was herself regarded as part of the inherited property; with this state of affairs we may contrast the provisions of the Code of Hammurapi, whereby the widow retained her dowry and the gifts made to her by her late husband. Daughters likewise had no right of inheritance in the Old Testament, except if there were no sons to inherit.

The childless widow, if not taken in marriage by her late husband's brother in accordance with the levirate law, returned to her father's house and might marry again: this custom is vouched for by the first chapter of the book of Ruth.

Commercial activity in ancient Israel was much more limited in scale and primitive in organization than in Mesopotamia, where the Code of Hammurapi and other legislation presuppose a relatively high degree of industrial and commercial development. Buying and selling was carried on in a very simple fashion, and it does not seem to have been necessary, as in Babylonia, to draw up a written contract. The first such contract mentioned in the Bible is in so late a source as Jeremiah (32, 9—12).

In the absence of written contracts, however, witnesses were indispensable as an effective guarantee of the observance of the verbal contract.

Loans and credit are treated in the ancient Hebrew system in a very elementary fashion, such manners of commercial operation being highly uncongenial to the character of the people. Generally speaking, Hebrew legislation in such matters shows a tendency to protect the poor on grounds of religious and moral justice. Usury among Hebrews was simply prohibited, and loans on security were restricted to the mildest possible terms (Exodus 22, 25—27). Every seven years saw not only the freeing of all Hebrew slaves, but also the remission of all debts.

There is very little certainty as to the extent to which these provisions were put into practice, but the protests raised by the prophets show that infractions of them were by no means rare. Jeremiah gives us a characteristic example when he relates how under king Zedekiah, after the liberation of the Hebrew slaves, their masters subjected them once more to servitude (Jeremiah 34, 8—11).

In Hebrew criminal law, especially in its more ancient phase, the forms of private law still prevailed to a large extent; the exaction of a penalty was often left to the direct action of the injured party, who could also waive his rights.

The "Book of the Covenant" explicitly formulates the law of retaliation as the fundamental principle of penal law. This principle, repeated and confirmed in other parts of the Hebrew body of law, is derived from the custom that prevailed in the primitive tribal organization, and, as we have already seen, came through the Code of Hammurapi to establish itself in ancient Near Eastern legislation. It is connected with the principle of collective responsibility, in that the entire family (or clan or tribe, as the case may be) is involved in the duty of avenging one of its members for a wrong done by a person not belonging to the group. God himself punishes sin, even in the sinner's posterity, just as he in even larger measure rewards virtue.

The law of retaliation is mitigated by allowing the injured party to accept the payment of damages. This alternative is explicitly excluded in the case of homicide (Exodus 31, 35), but involuntary homicides might profit by the right of sanctuary. Not only was such sanctuary offered by all sacred buildings and precincts, but the book of Deuteronomy (19, 3) mentions the institution of cities of refuge offering a like protection. The avenger of an intentional homicide had the right to demand that the murderer be expelled from his place of refuge; but, as the book of Numbers lays down explicitly (35, 22—25), the avenger may not, if the murderer has found sanctuary, take the law into his own hands by being judge in his own case; the community must decide whether the killing was really murder or not.

As in the Code of Hammurapi, the law of retaliation did not apply in the case of slaves. Here the penalties are much lighter; but a master who maltreated his slave might be forced to set him free.

The penalties attached to violations of the right of property are remarkably mild, especially as compared with the frequency of the death penalty for this class of crime in the Code of Hammurapi. Thieves are obliged to make restitution, often of more than the amount of the theft, or, if they are unable to do so, are reduced to slavery like other insolvent debtors. Similar penalties are assigned for embezzlement.

The commonest form of capital punishment was death by stoning. The condemned person was taken outside the camp, in the nomad period, or outside the city, in later times, and the first stones were cast by the witnesses. Other forms of execution were rarer. There is mention in some cases of hanging, and in punishment for certain crimes the culprit was burned alive: so for the prostitution of a priestess or of the daughter of a priest, or for incest (Leviticus 20, 14). This last crime meets with a like punishment in the Code of Hammurapi.

Corporal punishments mentioned in the Bible, apart from those resulting from the application of the law of retaliation, include flogging, to which however a limit of forty blows was set (Deuteronomy 25, 1—3).

Fines likewise are commonly connected with the law of retaliation, in that they take the form of damages as an alternative to the application of that law; but they were also inflicted in certain other cases, as for the crime of calumniating a young maiden.

This system of penal law, taken as a whole, is remarkable for the absence of certain common features of modern legislation. For example, the penalty of imprisonment is unknown to it; imprisonment, as a means for the defence of society, is almost entirely absent from the juridicial tradition of the ancient Near East.

The Bible tells us that Moses himself was the supreme judge of his people, and that he appointed, from among the elders and chiefs of the various tribes, subordinate judges for various sections of it. During the monarchial period, judicial authority belonged to the king, who sometimes conferred it on the priests. After the division of the kingdom, the administration of justice in the kingdom of Israel was in the hands of local notables, whereas in that of Judah king Jehoshaphat reformed the judiciary system (2 Chronicles 19, 5—9) by the establishment in each city of a tribunal composed of Levites and lay judges, with a supreme court at Jerusalem. After the Exile, Ezra reorganized the administration of the law, which eventually came to be in the hands of the Sanhedrin.

Legal procedure was exceedingly simple. The judges used to sit at the city-gate; the establishment of a court of law in a room of the palace was an innovation introduced by Solomon. Contending parties presented themselves before the judge, and pleaded their own cases. Where there was no plaintiff, there was no trial; the machinery of the law was set in motion only "by request".

The judicial inquiry was carried out verbally, and the agreement of at least two witnesses was required for the establishment of the evidence. Heavy penalties were assigned for false witness, but for all that the distressing story of Naboth's vineyard (1 Kings 21) shows that it was not impossible to procure the condemnation of an innocent man by suborning witnesses.

The so-called "judgement of God", of which great use was made in Babylonia, is rare among the Hebrews. Traces of it are to be seen in the case in which a man accuses his wife of infidelity but can not bring forward proof of his assertion (Numbers 5, 11—30).

A passage in the book of Deuteronomy (25, 2) shows that penalties had to be inflicted immediately after the passing of sentence, before the eyes of the judge who had pronounced it.

ART

We have already seen how the religious prohibition of representation of the godhead hindered the development among the Hebrews of sculpture and painting. Something may however be said of architecture and of relief-work as representative of ancient Hebrew art.

Archaeological investigation has brought to light in several parts of Palestine the remains of citadels and of palaces: the citadel of Saul at Gabaa, excavated by Albright in 1922 and 1933; the much more elaborate and highly-evolved one at Lachish, where Starkey excavated from 1932 to 1938, and several others. The detailed archaeological study which has been made of Samaria merits especial mention here. In 1908—1910 Harvard University expeditions brought to light the royal palace, built in the form of a series of courtyards surrounded by rooms, that is to say on the same plan as the Mesopotamian palaces, but on a much more modest scale. The excavators were of opinion that the oldest portion of the building was to be attributed to Omri, the founder of the city, a later addition to Ahab, and a still later one to Jeroboam II; but the excavations conducted by Crowfoot in 1931—1935 showed that the constructions cover a much longer period: the oldest portion may be attributed to Omri and Ahab

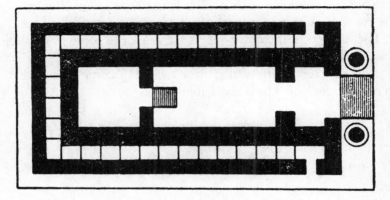

2. Plan of Solomon's temple.

together, the first addition to Jehoahaz or Jeroboam II, and the third to the hellenistic period.

As to religious architecture, the detailed description of Solomon's temple given in the Bible makes up for the lack of archaeological data. A gate flanked by two bronze pillars gave access to an entrance-hall leading in its turn into the central hall, rectangular in shape and containing the altar of incense and the table of shewbread. From this hall a curtained doorway led into the Holy of Holies, a dark cubical chamber containing the Ark of the Covenant. In the court in front of the temple were the altar of sacrifices and the great laver of bronze.

The most remarkable feature of Palestinian art was the relief-work on seals or on ivory plaques. Seals have been found in great quantities all over Palestine. The prevailing form is that of the scarab, borrowed from Egypt, and most of the designs are likewise of Egyptian inspiration: gryphons and winged sphinxes, winged scarabs, uraeus-serpents, winged solar discs. Animal figures are frequent enough, and include a magnificent specimen of a lion; human and divine figures are rarer, the latter being of foreign origin. The style is static and ornamental; the designs (usually only one on each seal) and the brief inscriptions giving the owners' names are mostly framed and separated by lines.

The subjects of the ivory-reliefs are similar to those of the seals. Such reliefs have been found by Crowfoot at Sam ri , in the northern sector of the walls; they probably come f om Ahab's "ivory house" of which the Bible speaks.

CHAPTER SEVEN

THE ARAMAEANS

TO the north of the Arabian desert lies a broad strip of land interposed between Canaan and Mesopotamia, and extending to the outermost southern bastions of the Anatolian mountains. This intermediate zone played at one time an important part in the history both of Canaan and of Mesopotamia. For Canaan it acted in turn as a confining and as a balancing force in the play of short-range politics; for the Mesopotamian powers, it represented the road to the sea, and the gateway to Palestine and Egypt. Such a region could not see the rise of any great or lasting native political power; like the rest of the Syropalestinian area, it was a place of passage for military and cultural movements.

The bold marauders of Semitic stock who are already attested from the second millennium before Christ as occupying Upper Syria and thence raiding the neighbouring regions played the part assigned to them by geographical conditions. Without ever developing beyond the status of little local kingdoms, they expanded during the period of decline of Mesopotamian power, and were overwhelmed in the ensuing reconquest. At a later period, after they had lost their independence, it was their singular fortune to play an essential part in accomplishing the one positive function allowed to them by the geographical conditions of their land, namely that of affecting, and transmitting through the medium of their widely-diffused language, a synthesis of the civilization of the surrounding regions.

HISTORY

Aramaean sources for the more ancient period of history are

rare; they consist of a number of inscriptions, for the most part recently discovered, belonging to the ancient sites of Guzana (the present-day Tell Halaf), Sam'al, Arpad and Hama.

Indirect sources are more plentiful, in the first place cuneiform texts recording the movements of the Aramaeans and the pressure exerted by them on the frontiers of the Mesopotamian states; from another quarter, the Bible records the Aramaean contacts of the Hebrew people in the various stages of its history, and preserves, in its more ancient accounts and genealogical lists, the tradition of an original blood-relationship between the two peoples. The period of the monarchy is especially rich in information about the Aramaean states, who repeatedly play a part in the political history of the Hebrew kingdoms.

The word "Aram", as the name of a region or of a state, first appears in the twenty-third century before Christ, in a cuneiform inscription of the Akkadian king Naram-Sin; from the context this Aram would seem to be situated in Upper Mesopotamia. The interpretation of this inscription is not absolutely certain; but a new mention of "Aram" is to be found soon afterwards on a tablet from the commercial archives of Drehem, belonging to about 2000 B.C., and referring to a city and a state near Eshnunna, on the lower Tigris. Another Drehem tablet, a few years later in date, contains the personal name Aramu, and the same name is found again in a Mari text of about 1700 B.C.

These are our most ancient references to the Aramaeans, obviously insufficient to allow us to trace their early history, but sufficient to demand a revision of the once received opinion that that history begins in the fourteenth century before Christ.

It is true, however, that more precise information is forecoming for the second half of the millennium. An inscription of the Assyrian king Arik-den-ilu speaks of victories over the hosts of the "Akhlamu", and this name reappears under subsequent kings, until Tiglath-pileser I announces that he has routed the

Akhlamu-Aramaeans who came from the desert to infest the banks of the Euphrates. The word "Akhlamu" may mean simply "confederates", and it would seem that the Aramaeans formed part of that confederation. After Tiglath-pileser I there are several other references in Assyrian sources to Akhlamu and Akhlamu-Aramaeans, but the simple term "Aramaeans" becomes more and more usual, and finally is the only one in use.

The Assyrian inscriptions which have just been mentioned are at one in the picture they give of the ancient Aramaeans: like the other Semitic peoples they make their first appearance in history as nomads, whose movements correspond to the periodic passage of the beduin from the outskirts of the desert into the settled regions. As for the direction of their thrusts, the main lines of their expansion were limited by the presence of already firmly established Semitic populations in the east and in the west, in Mesopotamia and in Canaan.

The Aramaeans attained their highest degree of political importance in the eleventh and tenth centuries before Christ, thanks to the decline of the Assyrian empire during that period. To the east, the Aramaean tribes invaded northern Mesopotamia, and founded there a series of little states, the chief of which were those of Bit Adini, with Borsippa for its centre, and Bit Bakhyani, with Guzana (Tell Halaf) as centre. Further to the south, several groups penetrated into central and southern Mesopotamia: here an Aramaean usurper, Adadaplaiddin, seized at the beginning of the eleventh century the throne of Babylonia, and on the shores of the Persian Gulf Chaldaean tribes, related to the Aramaeans, founded several little states, the most important of which was that of Bit Yakini.

On the other front of Aramaean expansion, to the west, there arose at this time in Cilicia the state of Sam'al. In Syria was founded, around Arpad and Aleppo, a state which took the name of Bit Agushi; at Hama, Ingholt's excavations have brought to light an Aramaean stratum belonging to about 1000 B.C.; and further to the south other states were formed on the borders of the Hebrew kingdoms. It is of these last states, thanks to the Old Testament, that we have the fullest information: chief of them were Soba and Damascus, which were conquered by David, but regained their independence after the kingdom split into two.

The Aramaeans' force of expansion, which stands out so clearly in this period, was not, however, accompanied by the ability to organize their conquests, or even, in general, their own states. The Aramaeans never made up an effective political unity, and their division into little local kingdoms, which was further determined by the multitude of heterogeneous elements with which they came into contact, was the decisive element of their weakness. The end of the tenth century before Christ saw the recovery of Assyria, and the beginning of the process of reconquest.

Assyria's first step was to clear the invaders out of Mesopotamia. This was done during the first half of the ninth century principally by Adad-nirari II, Ashurnasirpal II, and Shalmaneser III, who in 856 B.C. conquered the state of Bit Adini, the last stronghold of Aramaean power in Mesopotamia.

Shalmaneser next turned his attention to Syria, and after a series of incursions, inflicted in 841 B.C. a severe defeat upon a coalition of the Aramaean states, with which the king of Israel also had allied himself. The defeated states did not, however, lose their independence for some decades to come: to this period belong the inscription with which Kilamuwa, king of Sam'al, records his victories over his neighbours and the prosperity of his kingdom, and the stele erected by Zakir, king of Hama, to commemorate his success against a coalition under the leadership of Damascus. For all their boast of power, these inscriptions bear unmistakable witness to that incurable internal discord which was not the least cause of crisis for these little states.

In the eighth century before Christ, Assyria once more took up the offensive. In 740 B.C. Arpad, which the inscriptions found at Sujin show to have been the centre of opposition to Assyria, fell to Tiglath-pileser III. Next it was the turn of Sam'al, where a certain Azriyau had seized power and was raising an anti-Assyrian coalition; the usurper was conquered and put to death in 738 B.C., and the throne was restored to the legitimate king Panamuwa II, whose son Bar-Rekub records these happenings in his inscriptions. Sam'al was so brought within the Assyrian sphere of influence; archaeological traces of destruction by fire, and the cessation of all mention of this state in our sources, seem to indicate that it came before long to a violent end. Further south, Damascus was reduced to the status of an Assyrian province in 732 B.C.; Hama, after a last attempt at rebellion, was overthrown by Sargon II.

The political life of the Aramaeans went on for some time longer in Babylonia, where the Chaldaean tribes roused periodical anti-Assyrian agitation and even succeeded in coming to power with the Neobabylonian dynasty. In the centres of their direct political ascendancy, however, the end of the eighth century saw their final collapse before the westward drive of Assyria. From this collapse the Aramaeans were never to recover. Their independent history, an almost negligible detail in the great picture of the ancient Near East, so comes to an end, and Upper Syria, the seat of their power, passes successively under the rule of the great empires which succeeded one another on the Eastern Mediterranean coast. Nevertheless, the Aramaeans continued to exist as a people, and their language remained. The historical importance of the Aramaean states is but slight, as compared with the exceptional cultural importance which was to be assumed, in the course of the centuries, by the Aramaic language.

LANGUAGE

The end of Aramaean independence was the beginning of an

era of a new kind of expansion: the energy that had so soon been checked in the political sphere became transferred to that of culture. By a curious paradox of history, the Aramaic language, represented by but a few inscriptions from the period of political independence, now extended itself far beyond the confines of the Aramaean people.

The first phase of this linguistic expansion coincided with the period of Assyrian occupation. Aramaic, thanks to its much simpler form of writing, penetrated more and more deeply into the Mesopotamian world. Quantities of contracts, receipts and inscribed weights show how the use of Aramaic increased continually among the Babylonians and the Assyrians. Aramaic established itself also in diplomatic dealings, and took the place of Akkadian as an international language; for example, when the representatives of king Hezekiah were parleying with the Assyrian envoys during the siege of Jerusalem, they asked them to speak in Aramaic in order that the people might not understand (2 Kings 18, 26; Isaiah 36, 11); moreover, an Aramaic papyrus published in 1948 by Professor Dupont-Sommer, containing a letter from a Phoenician prince to the Egyptian pharaoh, and datable with probability to 605 B.C., bears significant witness to the westward spread of the new diplomatic language.

The greatest victories of Aramaic, however, were rendered possible by the Persian conquest. From the sixth to the fourth century before Christ the extension of Persian rule to the entire Syropalestinian coast brought about a temporary union of the North-Semitic world, and in the resulting levelling of culture Aramaic became the official language of the whole of that part of the Persian empire which lay between Egypt and the Euphrates. An official language of long standing tends to supplant the native languages, and in fact Hebrew, Phoenician and the other Semitic languages of the region were as time went on more and more superseded by Aramaic. One of the greatest difficulties in the way of Hebrew restoration after the return from exile was precisely the abandonment by part of the people of their original language.

During the Persian epoch Aramaic-speaking colonies penetrated also beyond the boundaries of Mesopotamia and of Syria and Palestine. Aramaic inscriptions have been found in various parts of Asia Minor, such as Cilicia, Lydia and Lycia, and also in Persia and in Arabia. In Egypt the Jewish colony at Elephantine has left us a series of Aramaic ostraca and papyri from the sixth and fifth centuries before Christ; and we have also documents on parchment, some of which, belonging to the archives of a Persian satrap of the time of Darius II, were published in 1953 by Professor Driver.

The advent of hellenism, with its cultural conquest of the Near East, produced a retreat on the part of Aramaic, but one that was accompanied by an advance in another sector, to the north of the desert, where the little preislamic states of Petra and Palmyra took over the Aramaic languages along with Aramaean culture. Moreover even for this period there are Aramaic inscriptions from Persia, from Cappadocia, and from Egypt.

The unification of the Near East under the Roman Empire, and later the spread of Christianity, brought about a recovery in the fortunes of Aramaic. On the one hand, it was adopted by new small states with Arab populations (so Hatra); and on the other, from being the language of Christ, it became the official language of the Syrian church, and as such was to establish itself for centuries to come and produce a great body of religious literature. Finally, there are traces of Aramaic-speaking groups throughout the western world; these were merchants and soldiers and slaves, who, among other things, brought about the diffusion in the Roman world of various Near Eastern cults.

The disunity characteristic of Aramaean history was naturally reflected in the Aramaic language, which consisted of a group of many dialects. A summary list of them will suffice to give an idea of their diffusion and of their division. From the more ancient period, we have the inscriptions already mentioned, the Aramaic of the Persian empire, and several passages in the Bible. About the time of Christ we can distinguish in Aramaic two branches. The first of these, called Western Aramaic, and representing an evolution which does not depart far from the ancient Aramaic, has several dialects: Nabataean, represented by the Petra inscriptions, Palmyrene, that of the Palmyra inscriptions, Judaean Aramaic, in the postbiblical writings of the Palestinian Jews (Targum, Jerusalem Talmud, Midrash), and Christian Aramaic, that of the Christians of Palestine. The other branch, Eastern Aramaic, differs more from the ancient form, and is represented by the dialect of the Hatra inscriptions, by Syriac, the language of the church of Edessa, with an ample literature from the second to the fourteenth century, by the language of the Babylonian Talmud, and by Mandaean, the language of the Gnostic group of that name.

Even nowadays there are in Syria Aramaic-speaking communities, and there are even larger ones in Mesopotamia and Armenia; but the Arab conquest led to the almost entire supplanting of Aramaic by Arabic. So Aramaic was to disappear, after having been for many centuries of vital importance as the vehicle of a cultural synthesis.

CULTURE

A great part of the historical development of Aramaean culture lies beyond the limits of this book. The Persian occupation, and above all hellenism, brought about the passage of that culture from the more properly Semitic sphere into a phase in which the loss of national independence was followed by the formation of an extremely composite civilization, with a multitude of trends of foreign origin. Though the Aramaean basis still remained, and in particular the Aramaic language was the vehicle of the new culture, that culture itself can no longer be called a predominantly

Semitic one. Similarly, the Christian literature in Aramaic is the product of a later cultural world, and has carried over into a different historical setting its elements of Semitic origin.

The very life of the Aramaean people is marked by its destiny as an agent of assimilation and transmission. This outstanding characteristic of its cultural expressions is evident above all in its religion, the product of the impact upon its national tradition of powerful influences exercised by the civilizations round about. At the same time, Aramaean political disunion inevitably excluded the development of religion on a common national basis, and gave to each city its own religious evolution.

There were for all that several deities whose worship was not confined to this or that city-state. This is above all true of the god Hadad, the equivalent of the Babylonian and Assyrian Adad, and, in his functions, of the Hittite and Hurrian supreme god. Hadad was in origin the king of the storm, and manifested himself in lightning and wind and also in the beneficent rain. The Greek writer Lucian tells us of his worship in his shrine at Hierapolis, to the south of Carchemish, with rites which certainly go back to an earlier age. He was likewise worshipped in Sam'al, in Aleppo and in Damascus, where three kings bear a name derived from his (Bar-Hadad, "Son of Hadad"). Being the sky-god *par excellence*, he was later identified with the sun-god. He was represented holding in one hand a thunderbolt and in the other an axe, and standing on the back of a bull, which was his sacred animal. As the sun-god, he gained admission also into the Greek and Roman worlds, which identified him with Zeus and with Jupiter.

Along with Hadad we find at Hierapolis a goddess named Atargatis, corresponding to the great Semitic fertility-goddess. This divine family was completed by their son Simios as the third member of the natural triad.

Canaanite gods figure prominently in the Aramaean pantheon. El is mentioned in Sam'al, along with the compound name

Rekub-El, and in Sujin with the name Elyon; and his name is an element in those of many kings. Baal is to be found in Sam'al as Baal-Semed and Baal-Hamman, and at Hama as Baalshamin, "Lord of the heavens". At Palmyra Baal (Bel) is the supreme deity; but the religion of Palmyra, as also that of Petra, will be dealt with in the next chapter, for the people of these little states were Arabs; their civilization, though Aramaean in language and predominantly so in culture, was of a mixed nature.

The Hebrew God Yahweh must also have been worshipped or at least known, since proper names are to be found in various places compounded with his name.

In the Nerab inscriptions there appear local gods, such as the moon, the sun, and fire, whose names and attributes point to Mesopotamian influence.

We have only a few indications on which to base a judgement as to the forms of ritual; these would seem to be similar to those of the neighbouring Canaanites, but beyond that we cannot go.

In conclusion, Aramaean religion follows the general lines of Semitic religious thought, and represents a complex growth in which there have been grafted onto the native trunk branches derived from the neighbouring cultures of Mesopotamia, Asia Minor and Canaan.

Little need be said of Aramaean literature for the more ancient period. Leaving aside the various historical inscriptions, including the funeral ones found at Nerab, we are left with only one text of this period which can be called in the proper sense a literary one, namely the story of Ahiqar, which has come down to us in papyri of the fifth century before Christ, but whose text probably goes back to the preceding century. The story is that of a wise and virtuous man, Ahiqar, chancellor at the court of the Assyrian kings Sennacherib and Esarhaddon. Having no son of his own, he adopts a nephew, Nadin, and passes on to him his high office. Nadin requites him ill, for by a calumnious denunciation he induces Esarhaddon to condemn Ahiqar to death. The executioner, however, connives at his escape, and he is able to rehabilitate himself by exposing his nephew's intrigue. To the story is appended a series of sayings attributed to Ahiqar, which are highly interesting in that they belong on the one hand to the tradition of ancient Near Eastern didactic literature, and on the other hand, make use of fables, a device which was to be developed in Greek literature. Here are some examples of sayings:

"My son, chatter not overmuch, utter not every word that comes into thy mind: men's eyes and ears are fixed on thy mouth. Beware lest it be thy undoing. Above all other things set a watch upon thy mouth, and over what thou hearest harden thy heart. For a word is a bird: once it is released none can recapture it . . .
The wrath of a king is a burning fire. Obey it at once. Let it not be enkindled against thee and burn thy hands. Cover the word of the king with the veil of thy heart. Why should wood contend with fire, flesh with a knife, a man with a king?"[1]

A fable:

"The leopard met the goat who was cold, and he said to her: Come, I will cover thee with my hide. The goat answered: What need have I of that? Do thou not take my hide! For thou greetest not, save to suck blood."[2]

The gist of some of Ahiqar's fables is repeated in the celebrated ones attributed to Aesop, and even Aesop's biography has been influenced by that of the ancient oriental sage.

The artistic production of the little Aramaean states was limited in extent, and, like Aramaean religion, shows a combination of Hittite, Hurrian and Mesopotamian elements, and even

---

[1] Ahiqar col. vii.   [2] Ahiqar col. viii.

Egyptian ones. There can be little originality, and the style depends principally on the political conditions prevailing at the given time and place.

The Aramaeans have left traces of their penetration into Mesopotamia in the culture of Tell Halaf, where von Oppenheim has found a large collection of statues and of pylons carved in relief. Aramaean work can be identified by its custom of representing the human face with the beard shaved above and below the lips. The subjects of the reliefs are mainly animal figures, fantastic beings, and hunting scenes, with a certain rough effectiveness. Naturally all this follows the main lines of Mesopotamian art, and may legitimately be included under that heading.

Of the Aramaean cities of Syria, Sam'al is perhaps the one whose hybrid character bears the clearest witness to the evolution brought about by the passage of time and the changes in the historical situation. Its architecture and its most ancient statuary are derived from Hurrian and Hittite models. The city was surrounded by a double line of walls, and in its midst was the acropolis with the military buildings, the royal palaces and the temples. A characteristic feature of the palaces is the colonnaded portico (*bīt khilāni*), which we have already met with in Assyria, and which, according to Professor Frankfort's studies, originated here in Syria. The entrance-gateway was flanked by two great lion-figures, with open jaws and pendent tongues; and there were many sphinxes. The statues of gods, kings and animals, which, as has already been said, began by imitating Hurrian and Hittite models, turn at a later period to Assyrian ones, even to the extent of dropping the traditional Aramaean form of the beard. To the Assyrian period belong the reliefs of Bar-Rekub, of which one represents him standing, and another seated, with a servant before him. The figures are awkward, and the positions of the bodies and of the arms are subject to the same conventions as in Mesopotamian art.

Damascus was in all probability the place of origin of a series of ivory carvings, bearing the name of "our lord Hazael" (which was the name of a king of Damascus), and found at Arslan Tash, near Borsippa, whither they must have been brought by the Assyrians as spoils of war. As was usually the case, the reliefs, while somewhat awkward in the human figures, were most successful in the animal ones, for example in those of a hind drinking, and of a cow suckling her calf. These ivories find an artistic parallel in the Hebrew ones from Samaria and Megiddo.

On the whole Aramaean art, before the hellenistic period, had a rough provincial aspect, though it was not without a certain creative spontaneity. It does indeed possess certain features of its own, but for all that it may be classified within the artistic tradition of Asia Minor and Mesopotamia.

Of the various forms of Aramaean civilization, the essential one is language. A language, however, is not an idea, or a cultural outlook, but only a means for the acquirement, expression and dissemination of culture; and in fact the Aramaean contribution to civilization consisted essentially in this process. The Aramaeans were not in a position to produce great artistic creations; their land was the clearing-house for the cultural productivity of the stronger states about them, and their language was the instrument of a work of cultural assimilation and dissemination, which goes beyond the limits of their local history, and becomes an element of Mediterranean civilization. The Greeks and Romans knew the Near East mainly through the Aramaeans, for it was they who united and canalized the sources of its culture, bringing together Babylonian, Persian and Hebrew elements and transmitting them to Christianity, and with Christianity to the West. From the West, at a later date, the Aramaeans were to bring to the East Greek culture, especially philosophy, which became known to the Arabs through the medium of Aramaic.

The ultimate foundation of the characteristics of Aramaean civilization was therefore, as we said at the beginning, the geographical situation; the land shared to an accentuated degree the fate, as an area of communication, of the Syropalestinian region, of which it was an integral part.

CHAPTER EIGHT

THE ARABS

COMPARED with the vigorous and changeful history of the northern Semitic regions, the picture presented by the Arabian hinterland is one of remarkable immobility. The desert which covers the greater part of the surface of the peninsula offers an obstacle to the movements of armies or traders, and preserves almost unchanged throughout the centuries the characteristics of its inhabitants and of the conditions in which they live. Hence, while on the one hand it seems likely that it was here that the Semites took on those features with which they first appear in history, and it is true that the Arabs have preserved, better perhaps than any other people, the most ancient of those features, on the other hand the inhabitants of Arabia make their own appearance in history at a fairly late period, thousands of years after the political establishment of other Semitic peoples.

The union of Arabia may be said to have been brought about by the great religious movement which was initiated in the seventh century of the Christian era by the preaching of Mohammed. The figure of the prophet thus marks a clear division in Arabian history: before him was dispersion and division, after him came solid political unity, and expansion far beyond the bounds of Arabia. Before Mohammed there were only small local states, along the trade-routes and on the fringe of the northern area, and the life of these states was limited in time as well as in space. The only exception — an exception in time, that is, because in space we are still dealing with small entities—was the south-western coastal region, Arabia Felix, where the excellence of the soil and the consequent possibility of settled culture

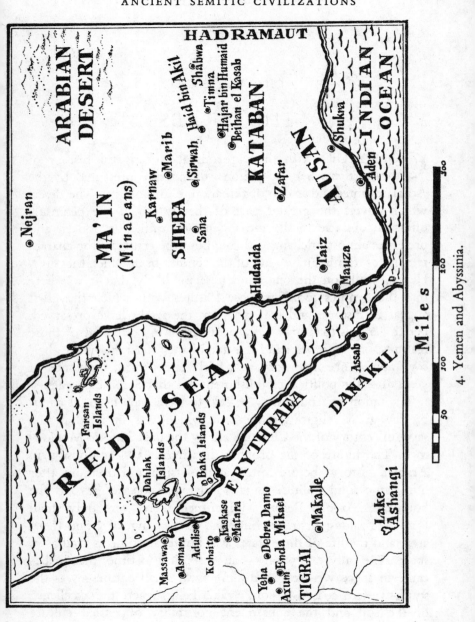

4. Yemen and Abyssinia.

permitted the organization of lasting and prosperous political units. This region had therefore a life of its own, until after a period of continual decline it was absorbed into the rising Islamic state.

Outside the settled groups, who were but a small minority, the beduin tribes passed over the desert in their periodic migrations in search of pasture and water. Unstable and changing as nomad life may seem to be to a short-term view, it is in fact immutable in the monotonous recurrence of its movements, year after year and century after century, and the whole region so takes on a static and isolated aspect as compared with the historical evolution round about it.

SOUTHERN ARABS

Our knowledge of Arabia Felix is still far from complete. Many problems remain to be solved before we can be sure of the history of the various states and of their relations with one another. Great progress has been made, however, since the first attempts, made towards the middle of the last century, at the decipherment of South Arabian documents. The voyages of Halévy and Glaser in the second half of the century brought to Europe a large number of copies and tracings of inscriptions, and since then the number has continued to increase up to about four thousand documents, while many more are to be expected as a result of the recent explorations carried out by the University of Louvain (1951—52) and by the American Foundation for the Study of Man (1950—53).

The inscriptions are in an alphabetic script which was probably imported from Canaan, although the letters do not bear much external resemblance to those of the North Semitic alphabets: of the known Semitic alphabets, they show an especial affinity with the Ethiopic. The language, or rather the group of various dialects, is likewise related to Ethiopic. The reason for this is clear enough: Ethiopic civilization is an offshoot of South Arabian, since Abyssinia was colonized by immigrants from the Yemenite coast.

The matter of the South Arabian inscriptions is made up of votive and sepulchral dedications, building-inscriptions, records of historical events, decrees, economic texts. From all this material it is possible to reconstruct lists of the kings and of the principal events in the life of each of the states, and further assistance is given by certain indirect sources. There is a very extensive pre-islamic Arabic tradition, but as this is for the most part legendary in character, it is poor in reliable material. Certain allusions are to be found in the Bible, notably the celebrated account of the visit paid to Solomon by the Queen of Sheba; Assyrian cuneiform inscriptions give us a couple of hints; and from the third century before Christ onwards we have important references in the works of classical historians and geographers, and in several religious texts in Syriac or Ethiopic.

In the first millennium before Christ various states appear in south-western Arabia. Outstanding among them are the kingdoms of the Minaeans, of the Sabaeans (Sheba), of Kataban and of Hadramaut.

The Minaean kingdom, in the northern Yemen, has been the most discussed from the chronological point of view. It was in the past uncertain whether it was prior to the Sabaean kingdom, or contemporary with it. Recent excavations, and the application of the radiocarbon process, point to contemporaneousness: the rise of the kingdom seems to be datable at about 400 B.C. The Minaeans are especially noteworthy for their development of trade with the north: they established important colonies along the Red Sea coastal route to Palestine and the Mediterranean. Towards the end of the first century before Christ the Minaean kingdom was absorbed in the Sabaean one, which had meanwhile been extending its power in the region further south.

Cuneiform inscriptions of the eighth century before Christ tell us that Sabaean chiefs and kings offered tribute and gifts to Assyrian monarchs. The Sabaeans in question must have been colonists in northern Arabia, a fact which indicates the flourishing condition of the state at so early a date. The most ancient Sabaean inscriptions show us, at the same period, a remarkably high degree of cultural development.

The Sabaean state evolved from a religious form of government to a secular one. At an earlier date its rulers bore the title *mukarrib*, which may be rendered "high priest". Towards the end of the period of the mukarribs the capital of the kingdom was fixed at Marib, where an enormous dyke was meanwhile being constructed to contain the river Adhanat and divert its waters for the purpose of irrigation. About the fifth century before Christ came the transition to a lay form of government, based on the oligarchy of a small number of military and landed families. At the head of the state were kings, under whom the Sabaeans progressively extended their dominion. At the end of the second century before Christ the kings of Sheba added to their title that of king of Raidan, and a new capital was established at Zafar. At the same time the tribe of the Himyarites began to take foremost place in the state, and their name, in the form Homeritae, is found with increasing frequency in classical authors alongside or in place of that of Sabaeans.

Towards the end of the first century before Christ, as we said, the Minaean kingdom was absorbed into the Sabaean. The same fate befell Kataban, whose history, according to the new chronology, is to be placed approximately between 400 B.C. and 50 B.C., and some time later Hadramaut, whose history, according to the same system of chronology, lies between 450 B.C. and the second century after Christ. The inscriptions of both of these states mention mukarribs, which leads to the supposition that their original form of government was similar to that of the Sabaeans. By the third century of the Christian era the Sabaeans had welded southern Arabia into a single strong state, the largest political unity formed by the southern Arabs.

This kingdom was soon fiercely attacked by the Ethiopians. In the fourth century it was for a while occupied by them; later it recovered its freedom, but internal dissension, due principally to the introduction of Judaism and Christianity, now began to send it down the path of decline. The Jewish element became stronger and stronger, and the last Sabaean king, dhu-Nuwas, attempted to impose Judaism on his people, and began a violent persecution of the Christians. This led the Christian Ethiopians in 525 to invade and occupy the Yemen.

Under the Ethiopian occupation the crisis became intensified. While the Christian governors were building churches, and seeking to thrust northwards with the celebrated Abraha (who is nowadays thought to have governed the Yemen as an independent sovereign), the country fell ever more and more into decline owing to the dying-out of the commercial activity which was largely bound up with its very existence. A development of the use of the sea-routes competed disastrously with the caravan trade, and finally in 542 the collapse of the Marib dyke brought devastation to the flourishing irrigated lands and dealt the death-blow to Yemenite prosperity.

Abyssinian dominion came to an end in 575, and was succeeded by that of Persia, which was finally in its turn to be supplanted, during the last years of Mohammed's life, by Islam.

The South Arabian inscriptions record a host of names and epithets of gods, which give us the impression of an extremely complex pantheon. The local character of the majority of the gods, and the custom of referring to them anonymously or by their epithets add to the researcher's difficulties. However, the existence of certain general conceptions, around which the multitude of gods can be grouped, is beyond doubt.

An astral triad, which we have already seen in Mesopotamia, is predominant in southern Arabia: the god of the morning-star, the moon-god and the sun-goddess. It would be an exaggeration to seek, as Nielsen did in his celebrated thesis, to reduce all the deities to terms of this triad, but it is true that it played a leading part in the South Arabian pantheon, and that many of the various divinities are but its manifestations.

The name of the star-god is common to the whole region: Athtar, a variant of the well-known Ishtar of the Babylonians and Assyrians, and Astarte of the Canaanites. Characteristic, however, is the fact that the South Arabian Athtar is a male deity, whereas all the other Semitic religions have a female one.

The moon and the sun appear under different names. The former, who is Wadd for the Minaeans and Ilumquh for the Sabaeans, is in Kataban called Amm, and in Hadramaut Sin (as in Babylonia); along with other names the sun has in Kataban and Hadramaut that of Shams, a form related to the Mesopotamian Shamash. Such correspondences confirm the interdependence, among the Semitic peoples, of many religious elements.

Alongside the common deities was a whole host of particular ones, patrons of places, of tribes, or even of families. These are often referred to simply as *ba^cal*, a name we have already met with among the Canaanites, meaning "master, patron". Not all these divinities came from the national stock; some were borrowed from neighbouring peoples, in accordance with an assimilative readiness common among the southern Arabs, which in the later phases of their history was to facilitate the introduction of Jewish and Christian beliefs.

The South Arabian pantheon contains many nameless gods, who are invoked, individually or collectively, by the use of such formulas as "the god" or "the gods" of a particular place or group of people.

Special mention may be made of Il, a name common to the entire Semitic pantheon: Akkadian Il, Canaanite El, Hebrew Elohim, Arabic Allah. The Yemenites also knew this name, and used it for the most part as a common noun, "god", which indeed it was in origin. It is occasionally found, however, as a proper name; and is very frequent as an element in personal names.

Theophoric personal names are the principal source of our knowledge of the attributes under which the southern Arabians were accustomed to invoke the gods. Among the commonest are the titles: father, lord, king, mighty, just, steadfast. Man's subjection is emphasized; a constant characteristic of this religious outlook is man's seeking after divine protection.

In Southern Arabia religion entered into every form of life. In consequence of the conception of the necessity of divine protection for the success of every being and every act, not only tribes and families, but also states and agricultural and commercial groups all had their tutelary deities. Propitiatory and dedicatory ceremonies were performed in connection with any activity of any importance. Temples and aqueducts, laws and official acts, funeral stelae, all were put in the care of the gods, who were to avenge any violation or profanation of them.

In such an environment, temples were of primary importance. Tithes and other sources of income were allotted to them in order to ensure ample funds for their maintenance. The upkeep of the temples was the task of the priests, who were numerous and well organized. Perhaps their functions also included that of emitting oracles in the name of the gods; but here our information does not permit us to be certain. The temple personnel also included sacred prostitutes. These were for the most part foreign slaves, who were offered to the gods and consecrated themselves entirely to their service.

Sacrifices were offered of various animals, including oxen and sheep, often in great numbers. There were also bloodless sacrifices in the form of libations and the offering of incense.

A very interesting institution was that of pilgrimages to holy places; the similar practice of central Arabia was later to pass into Moslem religious tradition. Similarly, although the practice of making the circuit of holy places is not explicitly attested, there are several indications which suggest that it existed in a form not unlike that which prevailed among the other Arabs.

Private prayer, in the sense of prayers not associated with religious functions or fixed hours, must have been widely practised. Its object was above all the imploring of divine protection and hence of fruitfulness for one's land, of success in one's trade, of freedom from want and from disease. Infractions of the conception of purity, which was highly developed in connection with ritual, were followed by public confession. We have examples of such confessions made by tribes to various deities, and of public penance on the part of kings.

Jewels, goblets, seals, and objects of every sort have been found in South Arabian tombs. This points to a belief in survival; but here, as elsewhere, we cannot ascertain the details of that belief.

As a whole, the religious life of southern Arabia is that of a highly developed settled culture with its own clearcut individuality and independence within its environment. It offers a contrast, very marked in many ways, with the conditions of the nomad Arabs further south.

It is not easy to build up a picture of the political and social life of populations who have left us no other records but votive and commemorative inscriptions. The latter are numerous enough, however, to allow us to draw certain cautious conclusions in this respect. On the other hand, the division of the region into various states means that in spite of the considerable degree of uniformity over the whole area, conclusions formed for one state are not necessarily valid without exception or qualification for other states.

The political organization of the South Arabian states took the form of strong, unified monarchies. The head of the state was the king, whose authority mainly underwent an evolution from the religious to the secular sphere. The recent studies of J. Ryckmans have traced for us the outline of political development in the Minaean and, especially, in the Sabaean kingdom. Here, under the rule of the mukarribs, the tribes formed religious communities under the patronage of their own deities; in his legislative functions the ruler was assisted by an assembly of the people. In the period of the kings the assembly still remained at first; special hereditary magistrates, whose title was *kabīr* ("Grandee"), saw to the administration of the law in each tribe. About the beginning of the Christian era, with the expansion of Sabaean conquest, the power of these Grandees grew increasingly until they became a privileged class within the tribes, with great territorial possessions; the popular assembly disappeared, the royal authority diminished greatly, and so there grew up a sort of feudal system. In military affairs authority seems at all times to have been in the hands of the ruler: the inscriptions recording warlike enterprises generally state that they were carried out at his order, and the assemblies do not seem to have had any say in the matter. From the religious point of view, Sheba seems, even in the period of the mukarribs, to have had a more secular type of government than the Minaean kingdom or Kataban, where the activity of the priesthood was more prominent.

The king's successor seems regularly to have been his son, or, failing that, his brother. A typically South Arabian institution, of Minaean or Katabanian origin, probably taken over by Sheba after its conquest of Kataban, was that of co-regency, whereby the king associated with himself in the government of the state the son who was to succeed him, or, at a later stage, several of his sons, including his heir.

The authority of the king and of local chieftains was ultimately founded on territorial possession; hence the administration of the state was based on landed property, and largely directed towards its interests. The temples likewise had their estates, from which a great part of their prosperity was derived.

We have some data about the fiscal administration. Taxes were levied on commercial transactions and on landed property, and there were special taxes for military expenses. The rate of taxation seems not to have been fixed, but to have varied according to the harvest and other factors.

In addition to its highly-developed agricultural resources, the economic life of southern Arabia was founded on international trade. In particular, Arabian perfumes were famous throughout the world: they were exported by sea or by the caravan-routes which led to Mesopotamia and Palestine. In the commercial field, southern Arabia also played an essential part as a centre of exchange. It was the landing-stage of the Indian Ocean for trade with the Mediterranean. The trading-bases planted by the Sabaeans on the coasts of India and Somaliland gave them a monopoly over the exchange of gold, of incense, of myrrh and of ornamental woods which those regions exported to the north.

Commercial interests and needs therefore penetrated the entire policy of southern Arabia: without any great political expansion it was able to reach far-off lands through its colonization and its commerce.

Southern Arabia has not yet been so extensively explored as have other parts of the Near East. The great temples and magnificent palaces whose memory is preserved by ancient writers still lie in part in ruins beneath the sandhills which for centuries have covered the remains of that vanished civilization.

Southern Arabia is rich in granite, which furnished admirable building-stone, from which great square blocks and strong pillars were hewn, while the extensive forests of ancient times provided timber. Brick was also used, and the frequent use of a step-formation in the capitals of pillars and in roofs recalls the similar features of many Mesopotamian buildings.

Imperfect as it is, our knowledge of South Arabian architecture permits the description of certain of its characteristics. The great stone blocks were so accurately finished and fitted together that the joins were often imperceptible. Even the pillars were firmly sunk into sockets in their bases and architraves. The walls are generally smooth, but we know that they were also built with ribbed surfaces. This technique gives the impression of having drawn its inspiration from brickwork, and on the whole recalls Babylonian architecture. A remarkable amount of care went into the adornment of walls and pillars with bosses of gold or of other metals, in which southern Arabia was rich.

Great use was made of pilasters and columns. Tall monoliths were erected, often bearing inscriptions. Capitals of pillars were often square, and sometimes multiple, superimposed in step-formation; the pillars themselves might be square or octagonal or sixteen-sided.

Temples were elliptical or rectangular in plan. A good example of the former type is the great sanctuary at Marib brought to light by the American mission. The precinct-wall, in the form of a rough ellipse, has been found, and a later construction built into it has been explored in detail. This edifice has a front with eight pilasters; an entrance of three doorways side by side gives access to a peristyle hall, from which a single doorway leads into the temple-precinct itself. A good example of the quadrangular type is the sanctuary of Khor Rory in Oman, also found by the American mission. The walls are extremely thick (ten feet and more), and within the northern wall three others have been added. There is but one entrance, and that a narrow one, set in the eastern wall. Within the temple-precinct there are two altars and a well fitted with a cistern.

Other buildings besides religious ones have also been brought to light, built of stone blocks or of brick: many-storeyed castles, walls and towers. A particularly important branch of civil architecture was the construction of dykes, one of which, that of

Marib, was of primary importance to the political well-being of the country. The excavations in the Timna zone have brought to light a whole system of dykes with canals and cisterns, ensuring the irrigation of a wide stretch of country.

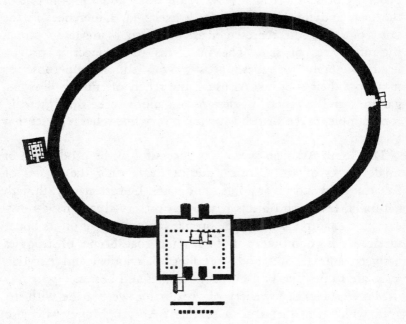

3. Plan of temple at Marib.

Sepulchral edifices were the object of especial care. Funeral chambers, mausoleums and stelae have been found, often bearing a portrait of the dead man and an epitaph. Stone tombs, hollowed out of the rock, with funerary furniture and yet more inscriptions, were found at Timna by the recent American mission.

Sculpture did not rise to such heights as did architecture. The prevailing type is that of small statuettes of persons, to be set in temples as votive offerings. Some fine bronze statues have been found, as for example that recently discovered at Marib, about three feet in height, of a man wearing a lion-skin on his back, or that of a horse, which is now in the Dumbarton Oaks collection at Washington; but in general this art is of a rough and primitive type. The same applies to the reliefs: human figures generally present a frontal view of the body and a profile one of the feet, and the faces are poorly executed. Differences in the status of the persons represented are indicated, as in Mesopotamia, by differences of size. The problems of perspective proved insurmountable for these artists, who simply superpose or juxtapose their subjects. As usual, the reliefs of animals, flowers, garlands and geometrical designs are more successful: there is, for example, in the British Museum a very fine relief representing a camel.

The South Arabians were very successful in the production of small works of art. Classical authors have sung the praises of Sabaean gold and silver goblets and vases. Unfortunately, though naturally, few such objects have been preserved; we have however, for example, a very fine bronze lamp, bearing on its upper surface a design in the form of a leaping goat. Scenes of struggles between animals and gods, recalling Babylonian and Assyrian seals, are to be found on bronze brooches and bosses.

Many articles of jewellery of great value were made with the gold which was plentiful in southern Arabia. Money was also coined in great quantity, a practice derived from the Greek world, whose influence is to be seen in the coins themselves.

In conclusion, the art of southern Arabia, like the other manifestations of the culture to which it belonged, gives proof of a remarkably advanced stage of civilization, prosperously and solidly established in settled conditions, and not merely independent of the rest of Arabia, but markedly contrasting with it in many ways.

CENTRAL AND NORTHERN ARABS

The history of preislamic Arabia, if we except the southern

region, is that of the vicissitudes of little political groups which arose in succession along the fringe of the desert, from the coast of the Red Sea to the edges of Palestine, Syria and Mesopotamia. Unstable in their structure and shortlived, these little states are in reality no more than a by-product of the process of contact and transition between the nomad zone and that of settled culture. They were not only the meeting-grounds and stage-points of the periodic movements of expansion originating within the desert, but at the same time the protective screen thrown up by the surrounding regions.

In addition, however, to this geographical factor, economic forces went to form the history of Arabia in ancient times. The peninsula is bordered, as we have already said, by two main lines of passage, along which merchandise travelled from the Indian Ocean to the ports of Palestine and Syria, following the edge of the desert. One of these trade-routes went from the Yemen into southern Palestine, and the other from the Persian Gulf entered the Mesopotamian valley and thence turned off into Syria, making for Damascus. It was along these routes that the little Arabian frontier-states grew up, and the operation or the closing of those routes, according to the Near Eastern political situation, determined the fate of those states.

Except in so far as they pass into these border-states, the nomads as such rarely appear on the historical scene. They are the inexhaustible reserve of the Arab people; with their infiltration into the settled regions and so into history, they cease at once to be wholly nomads, and yield their place in the desert to others who will in due course follow them over its borders.

Hebrew tradition, with its tale of the selling of Joseph by his brethren to Arab merchants, gives us perhaps the most ancient reference to these people, a substantially significant one, in that it is as raiders and caravaneers that the most disparate sources of antiquity mention the sons of the desert. The Assyrian annals for their part record, from the ninth century before Christ, royal expeditions against the nomad raiders of the northern desert. From Shalmaneser III to Ashurbanipal, Assyrian policy was directed towards maintaining the security of the frontier and of communications with the West, without however aiming at the permanent subjection of the Arabian hinterland. The bas-reliefs of Ashurbanipal's time give us pictures of these campaigns, in which we see the beduin fighting on camel-back, and their tents being burned. Several times there is mention of the names of queens, a remarkable fact, which has led to the supposition that the ancient tribal organization contained an element of matriarchy.

The periodic migratory movement from the desert towards the cultivated regions eventually led to the foundation, towards the fifth century before Christ, of the first unified state on the outer fringe of the Palestinian region. Its capital was Petra, an important stage-point on the trade-route along the edge of the Sinaitic peninsula; the American excavations conducted by Professor Glueck have now brought to light many other centres grouped around and dependent on Petra.

The people of this state, the Nabataeans, were largely influenced by the Aramaic language and culture, and so anticipated that meeting of the Arabic and Aramaean civilizations which was to be accomplished on so large a scale and bear such abundant fruit when the Arabs, united by Islam, set out to conquer the world. Moreover, more and more links are being found between the Nabataean civilization and the classical world.

Our earliest information on Nabataean history comes from writers of the hellenistic period. The Nabataeans were repeatedly brought into conflict with the Jews, and hence Flavius Josephus's history tells us much about them. Their state reached the height of its prosperity during the period which preceded the Roman occupation of Syria in 65 B.C.; during this period the whole region to the east and south of Palestine came under Nabataean rule, which extended southwards as far as the city of el-Hejr, now Medain Salih.

Further to the south lay another political centre, Dedan, now el-Ula, an ancient Minaean colony, and the northernmost outpost of South Arabian civilization; here there arose the independent kingdom of the Lihyanites, known to us from numerous inscriptions discovered in that region. This state reached its highest point of prosperity at the beginning of the Christian era or perhaps somewhat later. In the same area there are other sets of inscriptions similar to the Lihyanite ones, namely those called Thamudic, because attributed to the Thamud people, and those called Safaitic, further north, to the south-east of Damascus. The alphabet used in all these inscriptions is of South Arabian type.

The Roman conquest of the Near East marked for the Nabataeans the beginning of the period of decline: they came under Roman hegemony, and fell victim to the Eastern policy of Trajan, who in 105 A.D. turned the Nabataean state into the Roman province of Arabia. The Nabataeans have left noteworthy traces of themselves in all that region, especially by their development of the irrigation and agriculture of Transjordania; the extent of their commercial and maritime enterprise is witnessed to by the inscriptions found in the Aegean and at Puteoli.

The breakdown of Nabataean power led to the progressive abandonment of its trade-route in favour of the other one, that of the Euphrates, and this in its turn brought about an increase in the importance of the stage-point on that route between the Euphrates and Damascus: the oasis-state of Palmyra, which during the first century before Christ grew steadily in power thanks also to the diplomatic and commercial importance of its position between the rival Persian and Roman empires. Palmyra grew up, as Petra had done, within the orbit of Aramaean civilization, and adopted its language and the essentials of its cultural and religious thought, while at the same time it took much from the classical world. Its power went on increasing until towards the middle of the third century of the Christian era it extended over Syria and the Roman Near East; but Queen Zenobia's policy of independence and hostility to Rome soon brought it to disaster: in 272 the Emperor Aurelian entered the city of Palmyra and put an end for ever to its independence.

Like Petra, Palmyra left its mark on the Mediterranean world. Its merchants, and above all its soldiers, celebrated as bowmen, were to be found everywhere. Important and imposing remains of the city itself, along with those of nearby Dura, contribute notably to the reconstruction of its civilization.

The fall of Palmyra meant a temporary weakening of the protective screen between the desert and the outside world; the other little states of Arabian origin which were at that time in existence on the fringe of the Roman empire in Syria and Mesopotamia had no great defensive strength. The most important of them was Hatra, where the recent excavations (1951—54) of Dr. Naji al Asil have brought to light important remains of a composite type of art in which are combined classical and Persian elements. The historical life of Hatra lasted from the beginning of the Christian era until its destruction by the Sassanids about 240 A.D.

Meanwhile the nomads of Arabia were taking on a new vigour. The decline of the Yemenite states had given rise to a northerly emigration from that region of entire tribes in search of new lands, and the eventual result of this movement was that Petra and Palmyra were succeeded by newly formed little states along the outskirts of the desert. In the fifth and sixth centuries there flourished around Damascus the Ghassanid kingdom, and at the same time, near the banks of the Euphrates, the little Lakhmid state of Hira. These two states were dependent on the two great empires of Byzantium and Persia, constituting their advanced outposts on the desert frontier; but they declined and disappeared on the eve of the onslaught of Islam, leaving the empires face to face with the new invaders.

Even within the desert there were attempts at political organization, such as the state of Kinda, which united under its rule several central Arabian tribes. On the whole, however, the nomads remained free from all such forms of organization; united by blood-relationship into tribes, they sought no further unification, but wandered independently over their vast sandy home. Moslem tradition has preserved the memory of their rivalries and struggles: the so-called "days of the Arabs" are full of battles and vendettas originating in disputes over cattle, pasture or wells. Here the figure of the beduin stands out vividly with those contrasting characteristics of courage and pride and tenacity and guile, which were to play no mean part in the great organization to which Arabia was to give birth.

Cities had grown up principally at the oases of the Hejaz. The caravan route to the north was controlled by the predominantly commercial centres of Yathrib, later to be called Medina, and, further to the south, Mecca. Mecca was ruled by a merchant oligarchy. On market-days and religious feasts there poured into it groups of Arabs from all parts of the peninsula; as a place where the tribes met and mingled, no part of central Arabia was comparable to Mecca. Here was born Mohammed.

The social system of the ancient nomadic life has already been sufficiently described in dealing with the question of Semitic origins; it remains here to sketch the religious conditions of pre-islamic Arabia. The states which arose at various times on the outer fringe of the desert had each its own local religious development, dependent upon the historical conditions of its formation and existence. In the inner desert the nomads had by reason of their manner of life less opportunity to develop organized religious systems, and hence their religious life tended to be less intense, at least in its outward manifestations. On the other hand, Arabia did not remain untouched by the great monotheistic religions which grew up on its borders: Judaism and Christianity penetrated into the desert and provoked curious reactions, upon which was to work the preaching of Mohammed. Hence in dealing with the spiritual patrimony of the Arabs before the coming of Islam, one must speak of the religions of the Arabs rather than of Arabian religion.

An Arabian foundation, local elements, and Aramaean influences came together into curious syncretisms in the religions of the Nabataeans and of the Palmyrenes. At Petra the national god was Dusares, who was probably a form of the Semitic fertility-deity. His spouse was the Arabic "Allat", which means simply "goddess". At Palmyra we have the Semitic Baal, in the form Bel, which is of Mesopotamian origin, or Belsamin, "lord of the heavens", a name which we have already encountered in the North-West Semitic area, and which is to be found also in the Hatra inscriptions. Composite forms, which evolved, however, into independent deities, were Yarkhibol, Aglibol and Malakbel. It is probable that the form Bol is derived from an ancient local god, later assimilated to the common Semitic Bel. At Palmyra also we find Allat, and the astral triad common to so many Semitic peoples.

The Lihyanite, Thamudic and Safaitic inscriptions allow us to reconstruct certain elements of the religious system of those peoples. From the common stock they have retained the pan-arabic Allah and Allat, and to these they have added local gods, such as dhu-Ghaba for the Lihyanites, Ruda for the Thamudenes and Safaites. Finally, there are several South Arabian, Nabataean, Palmyrene and Aramaean deities.

The nomad tribes of central Arabia knew a host of divinities: not well-defined gods or goddesses, with their own established attributes and mythologies, but rather the spirits ruling and protecting each locality, somewhat after the manner of the various Baals of Canaan. The beduin imagination gave souls to wells and trees and stones, in which it felt the presence of the divinity. The famous black stone at Mecca, the object of veneration for the entire Islamic world, is but one of the relics of the ancient paganism, taken over by Mohammed into his new faith.

The desert was populated by other local spirits as well as the gods: a host of fantastic beings good and bad, possessing the power to become invisible; to escape from molestation by them, it was necessary to propitiate them. Mohammed, returning from an unsuccessful preaching expedition, relates that he converted on his way several of these jinns (Koran 46, 28—31).

The multitude of the desert divinities is a consequence of the state of dispersion in which the tribes lived, and of their predominantly centrifugal trend. Only in rare cases can a divinity overcome these influences and extend its sway beyond the limits of its own locality. Such was the case with the three goddesses Allat, al-Manat and al-Uzza, venerated around Mecca. Superior to them was their father, Allah. This last name, as we have seen, is properly a common noun, meaning "god"; it was widely used by the Arabs not only for the supreme deity in general, but also for various particular gods. Mohammed was to take over this name as that of the one God whom he preached.

The wells or trees or stones in which dwelt the spirits of the divine protectors of various places were naturally the shrines and the centres of the worship of those deities. The nomad manner of life allowed only a limited and rudimentary development of religious worship. In addition to the fixed local sanctuaries, there were also movable tribal ones. The latter were carried about with the tribe and were its palladium in battle. The ground about the fixed shrines was sacred ground. At the appropriate times pilgrimage was made to these shrines with song and music, and the pilgrims would run many times round the holy place, hurling stones or uttering religious cries.

There was no place in such a society for an organized priesthood. Sacred places were looked after by groups of families or tribes, but there was no reservation of the right to offer sacrifice or accomplish other ritual acts. A peculiar type of diviner, the *kāhin* (the Arabic equivalent of the Hebrew word *kōhēn*, which however means "priest") interpreted the will of the spirits by means of obscure oracles. These diviners also acted as judges and arbitrators. Another notable religious figure among the Arabs was that of the *sādin* or temple-guardian, whose functions were similar to those of a priest.

Only one religious locality among the many that existed in central Arabia was of more than local importance, namely Mecca. Its sanctuary, in which the black stone was venerated, was the goal of pilgrimages from many parts of Arabia. The situation of Mecca on the trade-route to the north made of it, as we have already seen, a commercial centre and a market-city. Commercial and religious importance together made it a meeting-place for the dispersed forces of the Arabs, and a beginning of panarabic centralization. This permitted the formation, in the religious and in the civil and commercial spheres, of a common national nucleus of tradition, which Mohammed was to turn to account in bringing about the political union of the Arabs.

Alongside the pagan tradition, the desert received also that of the two great monotheistic religions whose centre lay so near to its borders. Jewish groups migrated southwards, probably from the time of the Roman destruction of Jerusalem, and formed little colonies along the trade-route and at the oases of the Hejaz. Their principal occupation was agriculture, and they brought to their new home the religious and cultural tradition of their people. Their cultural level, modest as it was, must have seemed miraculous to the beduin, who looked on them with mingled envy and respect. The Jews for their part, though they adopted the Arabic language, held the Arabs in a contempt which was to prove fatal for themselves when they met Mohammed.

Christianity came into Arabia for a different reason and behaved in a different fashion. Its advent formed part of the general movement of the propagation of the new faith, and was motivated by a supra-national conception, thanks to which its penetration into new lands was not merely a matter of the migration of Christian groups, but consisted above all in the spread of the gospel. The northern Arabic kingdoms of the Ghassanids and Lakhmids embraced Christianity, and Christian colonies grew up also in the Hejaz, at Mecca, and in the Yemen, where they were in contact with the Christian Ethiopians. In addition to these lay Christian communities, there were the monks of the desert.

Arabian Christianity was not entirely orthodox; there were many monophysites, and representatives of various Gnostic sects. The Arabs were indifferent to doctrinal distinctions, and while they felt a certain admiration for the way of life of the monks and hermits, they knew little of their faith. Mohammed, for example, thought that Mary the mother of Jesus was the same person as Miriam the sister of Moses, and that the Trinity consisted of the Father, the Virgin, and the Son. It is not clear, however, whether these opinions were simply due to misunderstanding on his part, or whether they correspond to Gnostic doctrines.

Belief in the one God took a certain hold in preislamic Arabia. On the eve of the preaching of Mohammed, tradition tells us, there were a few men who professed monotheism. Their preaching served to prepare the way for the new religion that was about to arise. On the threshold of the new era, Arabian religion was represented by national traditions, Judaism, Christianity and monotheistic aspirations; only a singularly receptive spirit could have affected a synthesis of all these elements. Such a spirit was Mohammed.

The preislamic states have left their traces behind only in inscriptions, often short and hence offering but scanty material from a literary point of view. The inscriptions are for the most part commemorative ones, listing their subject's name and ancestry and occupation; there are also epitaphs, notices of proprietorship, and prayers. Their value is mainly religious, in that they record the names of various deities.

Within the desert, however, the nomads developed an independent poetry of their own, characteristic of their way of life and of their outlook on existence. These compositions have been handed down to us in the works of Moslem authors, and the important question arises, whether the latter are simply reporting them in their traditional form, or have added and invented on their own account. One may assume that at least a good part of this literature is the original creation of that heroic epoch of Arabian paganism which Islam called the age of ignorance.

The Arabs have at all times been connoisseurs of language; elegance of diction and pithiness of speech have always been reckoned by them among the highest virtues. From ancient times they must have had popular songs in crude rhyming prose, exalting the battles and the exploits of the tribe and of its heroes: a poetry of boasting and of daring, a poetry whose theme was man and his doings and conquests, man thinking and acting without any concrete religious sentiment to guide him.

The poet was a singular and attractive figure. He was credited with supernatural powers, and it was but a short step from the war-song to the oracle. Speech had magical power against the foe, and poetical inspiration was accounted a sort of magic, or a form of possession.

The Arabic poetry that has come down to us is not that of the first stages of literary evolution. It goes back no further than a couple of centuries before the advent of Islam, and its forms are so precise and stylized that it is reasonable to see in them the result of a long period of formation. The usual type of composition is one which consists of an indefinite number of lines, of which the first is composed of two rhyming half-lines, and all the others rhyme together.

These poems are usually constructed on a conventional plan. In the first part the poet relates his visit to the encampment, from which his beloved has departed, and bewails her absence; a theme rich in possibilities, but hampered by having become schematized and stereotyped in expression. Next follows the poet's journey across the desert, with its descriptions of wild nature. But neither danger nor solitude daunts the brave beduin: he reaches his goal and finds those whom he seeks. Then follows their praise—or their blame—which is the real object of the whole composition.

Into this general scheme various kinds of theme may be interwoven. Unhampered by any great exigence of unity, the poet follows his Muse down byways of description or reflection. This poetry strikes a strongly subjective note, in which the strange desert setting is seen transformed and coloured by the nomad's vision. Camels, ostriches, jackals furnish material for striking images painted with an unpretentious efficacy of expression which reflects the bare and obsessing simplicity of the desert.

A celebrated Arabian brigand, Shanfara, outlawed and persecuted for his crimes, has admirably expressed in a celebrated song the proud struggle against all manner of privation and hardship for the sake of an ideal of freedom:

"Somewhere the noble find a refuge afar from scathe,
The outlaw a lonely spot where no kin with hatred burn.
Oh, never a prudent man, night-faring in hope or fear,
Hard pressed on the face of the earth, but still he
    hath room to turn.

To me now, in your default, are comrades a wolf untired,
A sleek leopard, and a fell hyena with shaggy mane:
True comrades, who yield not up the secret consigned
    to them,
Nor basely forsake their friend because that he brought
    them bane.

And each is a gallant heart and ready at honour's call,
Yet I, when the foremost charge, am bravest of all the
    brave;

But if they with their hands outstretched are seizing
    the booty won,
The slowest am I whenas most quick is the greedy knave.

By naught save my generous will I rise to the height of
    worth
Above them, and sure the best is he with the will to give.
Yea, well am I rid of those who pay not a kindness back,
Of whom I have no delight though neighbours to me they
    are.

Enow are companions three at last: an intrepid soul,
A glittering trenchant blade, a tough bow of ample size,
Loud-twanging, the sides thereof smooth-polished, a
    handsome bow
Hung down from the shoulder-belt by thongs in a comely
    wise,
That groans, when the arrow slips away, like a woman
    crushed
By losses, bereaved of all her children, who wails and
    cries . . ."

"Bury me not! Me you are forbidden to bury,
But thou, O hyena, soon wilt feast and make merry,
When foes bear away mine head, wherein is the best of me,
And leave on the battle-field for thee all the rest of me.
Here nevermore I hope to live glad—a stranger
Accurst, whose wild deeds have brought his people in
    danger."[1]

Along with its merits, Arabic poetry has also its defects. The
stylization and artificiality of expression which it never shook off
often obscure the subjectivity of the inspiration, clothing it in
conventional garb. On the whole, however, Arabic lyric remains

[1]Quoted from R. A. Nicholson, *A Literary History of the Arabs*, London 1907, pp.80 and 81.

highly original; its strong and weak points alike are derived from the nature of the people who created it, for whom the desert was a home and a shelter from the vicissitudes of the civilizations which surrounded it.

Art does not flourish in the desert. In the northern states the arts were developed, but as their inspiration was predominantly hellenistic and Roman, they present little that can properly be called Semitic, and need be mentioned here only summarily.

At Petra, the frontages of tombs carved in the lofty rocks are striking for the vividness of their colouring. They are adorned with columns, pediments and porticos, and with rich decoration in the form of flowers and figures. Often they are built one above the other, even to the very summit of the cliff, and stairways are hewn to them in the rock. Similar tombs are to be found at el-Hejr, the caravan-station to the south of Petra. More interesting, because more spontaneous, is the art of the rock-carvings and paintings brought to light in the neighbourhood of Petra by Glueck's recent explorations.

At Palmyra a great part of the long colonnade at the entrance to the city has been preserved, as also the remains of temples. Here too, there is little originality, the style being mainly hellenistic and Roman. There are funerary monuments of three types, in the form of towers, of houses, and of underground vaults. The sculpture is largely in the form of relief, especially on tombs, and is dominated by the conventions of frontal representation, of immobility and of symmetry; it is this more than anything else which distinguishes it from its more advanced classical models. There are also some paintings in the sepulchral vaults, and some mosaics, characterized by the same features as the reliefs.

The art of Hatra, on which light has been cast by the recent excavations, is very similar, save that its temples and statues and bas-reliefs show a greater degree of Iranian influence, as was to be expected on account of the city's position.

MOHAMMED AND THE RISE OF ISLAM

The teaching of the prophet of Islam has been handed down in the Koran. This singular work, alone among the holy books of the great monotheistic religions, is held to have been written not merely under divine inspiration, but at the dictation of God himself; hence its spirit and its letter have at all times been deeply venerated.

Mohammed did not write the Koran himself; indeed it is doubtful if he ever learned to read or write. His words were taken down by his disciples on palm-leaves, sheepskins and stones, and, above all, were committed to memory. Hence when the first "bearers of the Koran" died in the struggle for the diffusion of Islam, the need was felt to fix in writing the whole body of revelation and so preserve it for future generations.

The official edition of the Koran was undertaken under the Caliph Othman in 650 A.D. The editors scrupulously respected the traditional text. Without in any way altering the sacred words, they simply arranged the various sections in descending order of length. This principle of arrangement accounts for the chaotic and inconsequential appearance of the resulting book, whose elements can however be sorted out by careful historical criticism.

The Koran exhibits a great variety of style and composition, from the brief, brisk and brilliant apophthegms of the first revelations to the tedious casuistical disquisitions of much of the later legislation; but it throughout faithfully reflects the spirit of its author, who had a marvellous power of transforming and adapting his thought to the changing circumstances.

In addition to the Koran, tradition carefully preserved as much as possible of the prophet's history. His biography, written by Ibn Ishaq, has come down to us in a later redaction by Ibn Hisham, from the beginning of the third century of the Moslem era; and a great number of his deeds and words were handed down from generation to generation and committed to writing by annalists and collectors of tradition. Unfortunately, the very admiration which the faithful had for the prophet led to the attribution to him of much that is unhistorical, especially in order to lend his authority to political movements or religious trends. The traditional material must therefore be sifted cautiously, and it is not always easy to distinguish between these pious frauds and the genuine matter.

Mohammed was born at Mecca into the noble tribe of the Koraish between 570 and 580 A.D. He lost his parents while still a child, and was brought up, we are told, first by his grandfather and later by an uncle. His youth must have been marked by insecurity and difficulty; perhaps he was a herdsman, perhaps he went with the caravans that left Mecca for Syria, where he is said to have received, from a Christian monk, his first notions of monotheism. It is certain that he had no first-hand knowledge of the Scriptures; even if he could read, they were not accessible to him in Arabic, and he certainly did not know Hebrew or Greek. There were however in Arabia scattered groups of Jews and Christians, who often came to Mecca on the market-days, and belief in one God was professed also, as we have seen, by isolated Arabs, who propagated it in their own circles.

When he was about twenty-five years old, an unexpected turn of fortune changed the whole course of Mohammed's life. The rich widow Khadija, in whose service he was, decided to marry him, and so freed him from the need to struggle for a livelihood. The marriage seems to have been a happy one; Khadija sympathized with her husband's aspirations and helped him to realize them, and he remained faithful to her as long as she lived.

When over thirty years old, Mohammed underwent the religious crisis which was to decide his destiny and that of Arabia. He went off in search of solitude. Islamic tradition relates how he retired to a distant cave and devoted himself to meditation, and there heard strange sounds and voices. One night the angel

Gabriel appeared to him and bade him recite, in the words which today form the beginning of one of the chapters of the Koran:

"Recite in the name of thy Lord who created,
Created man from clotted blood.
Recite, for thy Lord is most generous,
Who taught by the pen,
Taught man what he did not know."[1]

This first revelation was followed by an interval, in which Mohammed was a prey to deep depression; then came a new message from Gabriel (Koran 74, 1—7), and after that, more frequently, yet others.

He now began to preach; he converted his young cousin Ali and the Meccan nobleman Abu Bekr, and his message won him more and more adherents, especially among the humbler classes. So there grew up the first Moslem community, with the prophet as its uncontested leader.

From the beginning the idea of the one God occupied the forefront of Mohammed's mind, along with that of his own mission as the prophet of the Arab people. These two ideas formed the basis of his first preaching. To them was added that of the universal judgement, in which every soul shall receive the recompense of its deeds, the good shall be rewarded, and the wicked punished. Mohammed is come to give the final warning of this terrible event:

"When the heavens shall be rent,
When the stars shall be scattered,
When the seas shall be made to boil up,
When the graves shall be ransacked,
A soul shall know what it has sent forward, and what
   kept back.

[1] Koran 96, 1—5 (the Koranic extracts are quoted in R. Bell's translation).

O man, what has put thee wrong with thy Lord, the
  Generous,
Who hath created thee, and formed thee and balanced
  thee,
In whatsoever form He pleased constructed thee?
Nay, but ye count false the Judgement.
But over you are guardians,
Noble, writing,
Knowing what ye do.
Verily, the virtuous are in delight;
And verily, the scoundrels are in a Hot Place,
In which they shall roast on the Day of Judgement,
And from it they shall not be absent.
What has let thee know what is the Day of Judgement?
Again, what has let thee know what is the Day of
  Judgement?
The day when one shall have no influence on behalf of
  another at all, and the affair will then be in Allah's
  hands."[1]

The call to good works, to prayer and almsdeeds, is the community's defence against the impending event. Islam, like the
other great religions in their initial stages, did not make a sever-
ance between dogma and morals.

It was in the nature of Meccan society to react violently to the
prophet's preaching: to object to monotheism, which was infidelity to tradition; to repel the disquieting tale of a judgement; to
scoff at the claim to a divine mission unsupported by any tangible
evidence; and, not least, to be hostile to a religious revolution
which sapped at the basis of Mecca's honourable, and profitable,
religious ascendency. Mohammed had to meet the instinctive
hostility of a society whose principles were utterly at variance
with his own, a society based on that privilege which he

[1] Koran 86.

condemned, and aiming at the conquest of those good things in which he saw the cause of perdition.

Opposition to the new preaching penetrated into the prophet's own family, and one of his uncles, Abu Lahab, became one of his bitterest enemies. The prophet cordially returned his enmity:

"The hands of Abu Lahab have perished, and perished
    has he;
His wealth and what he has piled up have not profited
    him.
He will roast in a flaming Fire,
His wife the carrier of the fuel,
With a cord of fibre about her neck."[1]

Meanwhile controversy was sharpening the prophet's powers of argument. To his unbelieving fellow-citizens he replied by citing the examples of his predecessors, Noah and Moses and others, who were likewise in their day disbelieved and rejected; but those who disbelieved and rejected them were punished for their folly. To the demand for proofs of his mission he replied by pointing to the Koran: who, but one inspired, could have produced such a work? Such was the effect of the hostility of Mecca: as often in the decisive moments in the history of mankind, opposition served to harden the resolution of the young movement, and to force it to define and develop itself and take up a clear stand against all comers. This process has two great phases: that of Mecca, of which we have just spoken, and that of Medina, where Mohammed was to come into conflict with the Jews.

It was natural enough that the hostility of the Meccan ruling class did not confine itself to argument, but had recourse to persecution. Many of Mohammed's followers, mainly slaves, fled over the sea to take refuge in the Christian state of Ethiopia. This episode is not without its significance as indicative of the stage which had been reached in the development and definition

[1] Koran 111.

of Islam, as a movement which had made a clean break with paganism, but still looked upon Judaism and Christianity as its friends.

Mohammed himself most likely vacillated: the tradition that he one day uttered words of praise for the three Meccan goddesses, only to retract them next day as inspired by the devil (Koran 53, 19—23), is one which would hardly have arisen had it not been true. Nor was he at first successful in his preaching elsewhere. An unfortunate attempt to convert the neighbouring city of Taif ended with the prophet's precipitate flight.

The position was rapidly becoming more acute, and it was at that critical time that Mohammed came into contact with pilgrims from Yathrib (Medina). To them the idea of monotheism was familiar enough from their daily association with the Jews, and they were anxious to find a mediator who might put an end to the continual internal dissension with which their city was racked. They showed themselves inclined to embrace the new faith and accept and protect its prophet. Mohammed's genius saw and seized the opportunity; shaking off the dust of the past, he set forth in 622 with a few followers, for Medina. This was the Hejira, the decisive point in the history of Islam, and the beginning of its era. It was useless to expect any resolution of the crisis at Mecca; in the new environment everything might be hoped for. Mohammed's fortunes changed abruptly with this flight. From a persecuted visionary he became the respected head of a state, and his genius was equal to the task of mastering the new situation and turning it to his own ends.

The prophet's first task at Medina was to bring unity into an extremely unstable and faction-ridden political situation. The mutual hostility of the two local Arab tribes was tempered only by their common enmity for the Jews, who were numerous and influential. Moderate and conciliating in his impartiality, and gifted with uncommon diplomatic ability, Mohammed set about quieting dissension and turning the whole community into an instrument in his own hands. In a celebrated decree he proclaimed equality of rights for the various groups, and in the name of Allah appointed himself judge of all disputes. The establishment of his own authority was one with the introduction of a new bond of Arabian unity: upon the tribal system he superimposed a relig-ous principle which was to work a revolution of incalculable magnitude for the Arabs and their destiny, and weld them into a nation setting forth to conquer the world.

Now however there arose the second of the crises which determined the religious future of Islam, for Mohammed soon found himself at odds with the Jews. His slight cultural formation had led him to suppose quite sincerely that since he preached monotheism both Jews and Christians were his natural allies. He had made concessions to the ritual practices of the Jews, hoping in that manner to ensure their support; hence the introduction into Islam of the Kippur fast and of the custom of facing Jerusalem to pray, as the Jews did. Why then should not the Jews accept him as their prophet?

They showed no inclination to do so. Their irony, and their habit of posing difficult biblical questions, made it evident that they did not regard him as a prophet, and indeed wished to discredit him publicly. Mohammed reacted on the one hand by substituting the fast of Ramadan for that of Kippur, and prayer towards Mecca for prayer towards Jerusalem; and on the other hand, and principally, on the theoretical plane, by accusing the Jews, and the Christians along with them, of having falsified the Scriptures in which his mission was foretold. The argument was not a brilliant one, but it fixed Islam's independence of the other revealed religions, and its attitude towards them; having denounced Judaism and Christianity as falsifiers of the ancient revelation, Mohammed now showed that its genuine continuator was Islam, by declaring that the cubical shrine at Mecca, the Kaaba, was the first temple erected by Abraham and his son Ishmael, and that it was his, Mohammed's mission to restore the purity of primitive monotheism.

This argument convinced the Arabs and justified repression of the recalcitrant Jews. Now that he was sure of his power Mohammed threw aside his pacific and conciliatory attitude and showed himself cruel and relentless. The Jews were subjected to a violent persecution which reduced them to slavery and destroyed their community. From a historical point of view, apart from moral judgements, the anti-Judaic phase at Medina was the second of the crises that determined the independence of Islam, while the sad fate of the Jews was but another significant episode in the tragic historical destiny of their people.

Mohammed's ultimate goal, from the time of his flight from Mecca, had been the conquest of that city. With a grasp of strategy equal to his political insight, he realized that the way to bring Mecca to her knees was to strike at her life-line, the trade-route. In 624 a caravan coming down from the north was suddenly attacked near Badr by the Moslems. The army that was hastily sent out from Mecca was routed in spite of its great numerical superiority, and this initial military success set the seal to the prophet's prestige in Medina and filled the hearts of his followers with bold confidence.

This was soon to be shaken: scarcely a year had passed before the Moslems suffered a severe defeat at Uhud. Mohammed, as was his custom, righted himself at the expense of the Jews, and succeeded in this way in distracting the attention of his followers and minimizing the effect of the disaster.

Meanwhile Mecca was preparing an attack in force. In 627 a powerful army moved against Medina, but was checked by a trench which Mohammed had had dug around the city. When the besiegers gave up the attack and returned to Mecca, the defensive phase of the war was over for Mohammed, and the way to Mecca lay open before him.

Wisely, he bided his time, and negotiated. The treaty of Hudaybiya, though a disappointment for some of the Moslems, was the crafty prophet's political *chef d'œuvre*. The ten-year truce which it established would not hamper one so free from scruples as he was; and in return he gained the possibility of making officially in the following year the pilgrimage to Mecca along with his adherents. Mecca had consented to come to terms with the man it had persecuted and driven to flight; and in 629 he entered his native city full of honour and prestige. By 630 he had profited by the situation to such an extent that he was able to seize a pretext for breaking the truce, and enter Mecca as a conqueror, without a blow being struck.

Once more he resorted to a policy of prudent moderation. Instead of actuating plans of vengeance, he solemnly reconsecrated the holy places and passed off his conquest with piety. The people accepted with relief this peaceful revolution.

All Arabia was now falling before the prophet's feet. Taif fell, the Yemen fell; and the beduin tribes came one after another to do homage to the new sovereign. Mohammed meanwhile remained at Medina; he returned to Mecca only in 632, for his last pilgrimage. On the hill of Arafa, amid the emotion of his old companions, he announced that his mission was fulfilled, Satan would no more reign in Arabia. Soon afterwards he died. He had had the fortune so rarely accorded to great men of declaring his task accomplished on the eve of death.

What was there in the personality of this man, or in his message, which enabled him to remain master of events and bring about this singular revolution and shape the destiny of his people, welding the scattered states and tribes into a nation with a mission?

He was not the bearer of any great new ideal for mankind. It is not difficult to find in Judaism and Christianity and in the pagan traditions of his own people almost all that went to make up his preaching. His genius was not so much creative as assimilative.

Faced with contrasting trends, he brought them together, and his doctrine is essentially the result of a process of synthesis and accommodation.

Islam is a middle way. Set between nationalistic Judaism and Christian internationalism, it was Arab in origin and language, and in the privileged position of the Arabs with respect to their subjects, but it was international in its scope, addressing itself to and drawing within its fold peoples of every origin and, in principle, embracing the whole world. Set between monotheism and the pagan tradition, it adopted the principles of the one and many of the practices of the other, which it pressed into the service of Allah. Finally, while pointing heavenwards, it did not forget the earth. Unlike his more ascetic predecessors, Mohammed was a man with vices and passions, who keenly appreciated the good things of this world, and found a place for them in his religion.

Thus Islam, however revolutionary in its effects, is essentially a religion of compromise. Its very mediocrity, regarded by many as a defect, was, perhaps not so paradoxically, the primary cause of its success, in the hands of a genius.

The man who built up Islam must have been a politician of the greatest natural ability. Adapting himself to every circumstance, he was by turns cautious and daring, merciful and cruel, sincere and deceitful. His intuition enabled him to seize the most expedient course of action and apply it at the most favourable moment, and to make the most of each turn of events. In everything he was moved by the tenacious resolution to accomplish his own mission: he was as unwaveringly persevering in his aim, as he was flexible in the choice of means to attain it.

Of his initial sincerity there can be no doubt: the short and impassioned revelations of the Meccan period have the authentic ring of enthusiastic spontaneity. Later this sincerity became more sophisticated; but in judging Mohammed we must take into account his point of view: convinced as he was that he was the messenger of the truth, he subordinated all other considerations to its propagation and triumph.

His character was full of light and shade. Sensuality, cruelty and deceitfulness he had from his environment; they were the defects of the people whose son he remained; and though the ideal which illuminated him was an exalted one, the difficult conditions in which he was called upon to realize it forced him to adapt himself to them. Mohammed was the genius of the middle way; other prophets have had greater human qualities, but no other could have done for Arabia what he did.

Mohammed's death plunged Islam for a while into political crisis. Abu Bekr's caliphate brought into operation the expansionist tendency, whereby the young state, after settling its internal difficulties, moved resolutely beyond the frontiers of Arabia. Raids on the frontiers of the great empires to the north met with so little resistance that they assumed the form of an ever more ambitious movement of permanent conquest, which during the decade of Omar's caliphate (634—644) advanced at a headlong pace. Palestine, Syria, Egypt, Mesopotamia and parts of Persia fell in turn before the Moslem armies. At the beginning of the following century the Arabs had crossed central Asia and were at the gates of Chinese Turkestan, while in the west they advanced along the African coast and reached Spain, which they invaded and overran, penetrating into France, where finally their advance was checked by Charles Martel at Poitiers (732).

This gigantic eruption of forces that had lain dormant since the beginning of history, this overwhelming of the declining powers of the ancient empires by the fresh vigour of the desert nomads, united under the banner of their new faith, was a phenomenon which carried the Arabs beyond the limits of strictly Semitic history. In passing the frontier of Arabia, the Moslems opened a new historical era, in which Islam was to transcend national boundaries. New territories were annexed and new converts made.

Within the newly won empire were many ethnical and cultural elements of varied origin, which were taken up by the new religious unity into the formation of the history and culture of the new state. The great forces of Greek and Roman civilization and of Iranian tradition penetrated into the Arab world through Aramaic, which continued in this manner its function as a purveyor of culture. It speaks well for the modest Arab people that so far from being overwhelmed by this influx of the traditions of ancient civilizations, they were able to become the bearers of the new cultural synthesis. Through its language and its political privilege, and in many spheres of thought and art, the Semitic Arab element left its mark on the great empire to which it had given birth. Accepting what the surrounding world had to offer, the Arabs accomplished a work of assimilation and organization which showed them worthy heirs of their prophet.

CHAPTER NINE

THE ETHIOPIANS

ABYSSINIA

Over against the coast of southern Arabia, across the few miles of the Red Sea, lies the coast of Africa. This zone is mainly moorland, with green patches of pasture where there is water, but towards the south the desert prevails in the Dankali country, which to its own inhabitants seemed a veritable hell on earth.

Further towards the interior, the landscape changes abruptly. Above the plain tower the lofty precipices of mountain walls running from north to south, and descending gradually westwards. The plateau so formed, which in some places attains altitudes of over 14,000 feet, is deeply furrowed by the river-valleys; its steep cliffs form natural fortresses extremely difficult of access.

The climate and the vegetation of the table-land are in complete contrast with those of the coastal strip. In the summer months, while the lowlands are dry and parched, rain falls plentifully upon the mountains, and the lowland-dwellers migrate towards the interior.

The Abyssinian mountains are a place of refuge and isolation, in which ethnic, linguistic and political groups can shut themselves up and develop individual and independent forms of civilization, and in which political power and independence can build itself up and maintain itself throughout the centuries.

HISTORY

For the ancient history of Abyssinia we have both local and outside sources. The local sources include South Arabian inscriptions found in Ethiopia, Ethiopic ones, and Greek inscriptions of the sovereigns of Axum. The outside sources include South Arabian inscriptions found in the Yemen and recording events in which a part was played by the Axumites from across the Red Sea; writings of classical geographers and chroniclers, often based on personal visits to Ethiopia; and finally Islamic tradition, which however, as for southern Arabia, must be used with great circumspection.

The interests of international commerce which ruled the policy of the southern states of Arabia inevitably directed their activities to the Ethiopian coast, and the riches of the African continent—slaves, ivory, incense—were a strong added incentive to conquest and permanent colonization.

So it came about that at a remote period, and certainly by the first half of the first millennium before Christ, groups of southern Arabs crossed the Red Sea and established colonies and trading-stations on the opposite coast. Periodic thrusts in the direction of the zone of which the centre was the city of Adulis brought about a continual extension of the colonized area, and nature itself drove the colonists towards the desirable table-land. South Arabian inscriptions found in the Axum region and to the east of it, where the road from Adulis passed, show by the sixth century before Christ how far Arabian influence had spread in Ethiopia.

Whether all the Semitic colonization of the region was of Yemenite origin is another question. In the past no doubts were entertained in this respect, and on the Yemenite coast were identified the places of origin of tribes such as the Habashat, from whom the name of Abyssinia is derived, and the Geez, whose language predominated among the Semitic population of Ethiopia. Nowadays however, certain scholars have questioned the prevailing view, pointing out that there is no solid proof of its accuracy, and suggesting that the facts may be accounted for by South Arabian influence exerted upon a Semitic population already established in Ethiopia. Such a possibility cannot be rejected *a priori*; but it is not easy to see whence that Semitic population could have come.

A South Arabian inscription on an altar, recently found in Tigrai by the archaeological mission of the Ethiopian government, and attributed to the fifth century before Christ or a little later, mentions a mukarrib who was in all probability a local one. If this is so, there was already at that time a local state. Shortly afterwards the first Ethiopic inscriptions begin, in a script which is still in a transitional stage; and a bronze votive offering from the first century before Christ, also found in the excavations just referred to, bears the name of one Geder (if that is the correct vocalization of the consonants of the inscription) "king of Axum", which shows that that city was already the centre of the Ethiopian state.

Additional information about this state is to be found, from the same period, in the "Periplus of the Red Sea", a Greek composition of principally geographical character, which describes the gate of Adulis, and mentions, at a distance of eight days' journey from it, the capital of the Axumites, as a great centre of the ivory trade. The author of the "Periplus" adds that Axum was ruled by one Zoscales, a miserly man greedy for riches, well versed in the Greek language.

Our next information comes from a Greek inscription of the second or third century of the Christian era, mentioning "the king of the Axumites, the great Sembrutes". It is not clear whether it is to this king or another that we must attribute the great enterprises spoken of in another Greek inscription, that of what is called the Adulis monument, which we have in a copy made by Cosmas Indicopleustes, of which the beginning is unfortunately missing. The inscription is attributed to the third century, and the Axumite expeditions of which it speaks are on a truly grandiose scale, penetrating northwards towards Egypt, southwards into Ethiopia, and westwards in the Yemen. This far-reaching policy of the Axumites may find confirmation in the presence, attested by the historian Vulpinus, of their soldiers in the army which Queen Zenobia of Palmyra put into the field against the Romans.

At the turn of the third century of the Christian era, Axumite expansion attained important territorial conquests on its principal fronts; on the one side, the Yemen was occupied for some decades, as is seen from the titles of overlordship assumed by the kings in their inscriptions; on the other, the kingdom of Meroe was invaded and laid waste, as is shown by the fragments of a Greek stele found in that city. Meanwhile other names of kings are supplied by coins; among them is Ezana, who came to the throne about 325 and has left us both Greek and Ethiopic inscriptions, recording various undertakings, of which the most important was the expedition into Nubia.

When Ethiopia was so at the height of her territorial expansion, there took place a revolutionary event: Christianity, brought according to legend by two travellers, penetrated into the kingdom, and with the conversion of the sovereign became the state religion. Ezana, who had dedicated his earlier inscriptions to pagan gods, begins the last one, which records the Nubian expedition, with the words: "By the power of the Lord of Heaven, who is in heaven and on earth, the conqueror of all men."

It is uncertain whether the king's conversion was influenced by political motives; however that may have been, it had the advantage of favouring closer relations with Byzantium, the natural protector of all the Christians of the East. At the same time, the christianization of Ethiopia sharpened its rivalry with the non-Christian Yemen; and the crisis between Abyssinia and southern Arabia was in fact precipitated by religious considerations. The persecution of the Yemenite Christians by a Jewish king, which gave rise to an extensive Christian tradition in the stories of the martyrs of Najran, and which is also attested by Arabic writers, provoked the intervention of the Ethiopians. The expedition was commanded by King Kaleb, and its preparations at Adulis were witnessed by Cosmas Indicopleustes. It soon gave place to permanent occupation.

Southern Arabia fell under Axumite rule in 525. The conquerors left their traces behind them in the form of the Christian churches which they built, and in the fame of their attempted expedition northwards, probably with a view to taking part in Byzantium's struggle against Persia. This expedition, organized by the governor Abraha acting as an independent ruler, did not get very far, but it did make a great impression on the Arabs, who remembered it as the "expedition of the elephant"; and Mohammed refers to it in a chapter of the Koran. After Abraha, Islamic tradition records the governorship of his son Yaksum, whom it represents as a cruel tyrant.

The Ethiopian occupation of the Yemen was but an episode in the periodical struggle between Persia and Byzantium. It originated as such, and as such it came to an end in 572 with the Persian occupation. That was a fatal year for the Axumite kingdom; it marked the end of its conquests in Arabia, and of all expansion in that direction.

Islam, when it first arose, was in no wise ill disposed towards Ethiopia; on the contrary it is well known that Mohammed was on the best of terms with the Negus, and that the latter received hospitably the Moslems who fled from persecution in Mecca. When however Islam established itself as a political power on the western coast of Arabia and on the islands of the Red Sea, it thereby barred the road to any further Ethiopian immigration or influence, and a few years later, by invading Egypt and North Africa, it set up a like barrier between Ethiopia and the rest of Eastern Christianity. The Abyssinian state was thus cut off from the rest of the Semitic world, and shut itself up more and more in a purely local African policy. Its expansionist aims had now to find another outlet, and turned in a decisive manner towards the south. At this point we must leave the history of Ethiopia.

RELIGIONS

The most ancient religion of the Semitic population of Ethiopia was a form of paganism which, though it possessed various South Arabian elements, developed for the most part independently, evolving and assimilating other forms of worship. The god Athtar, proper to the southern Arabs, but going back to a Semitic stock common to other peoples as well, appears in Ethiopia as Astar, and gradually comes to stand for the sky, by analogy with the chief deity of the Cushitic pantheon. Alongside Astar there was Meder, mother earth, and Mahrem, the national war-god. These form, in some inscriptions, a triad, but they are joined also by Beher, taken by some to be the sea-god, and by others to be a variant of Mahrem. Minor deities and spirits completed the pantheon of Ethiopian religion, coloured and diversified by a series of local and imported elements.

Along with the pagans there were groups of Jews in Abyssinia probably long before the introduction of Christianity. Perhaps they came in groups from Arabia at the time of the first colonizing movement, or they may have come from Egypt, across the Meroitic kingdom. In the middle ages the Jews were congregated in the zone to the north of Lake Tana, where they continued to dwell for centuries, holding out against every form of pressure, and preserving their religious tradition even when they were no longer distinguishable from their neighbours in language or physical appearance.

In the Church History of Rufinus, who lived around the end of the fourth century and the beginning of the fifth, we have the oldest account of the introduction of Christianity into the kingdom of Axum. A group of sailors, on their way back from a voyage to India, landed on the Red Sea coast. The local inhabitants slew all of them save two brothers, named Frumentius and Edesius, who were carried off as slaves to the royal court. This took place about the year 320. The two brothers came to be well looked upon at court, and important charges were entrusted to them. Their first religious success was the obtaining of freedom of worship for themselves and for the Greek merchants who visited the country. In this manner the foundations were laid of a little Christian community, and the patriarch of Alexandria consecrated Frumentius as its first bishop.

It is probable that the conversions made by Frumentius were not numerous and were confined to court circles; but what was decisive for the history of Christianity in Ethiopia was the conversion of King Ezana himself, which made it the state religion. The fact of this conversion is confirmed by inscriptions and the symbols on coins; though it may have been but superficial, it was destined to have far-reaching effects on the international relations of the kingdom of Axum.

Abyssinian Christianity was doubtless at the outset orthodox, but along with the patriarchate of Alexandria it passed into monophysitism. Most probably monophysite were the famous "nine saints" of tradition, who came from Syria and carried on a great apostolate by means of the translation and diffusion of sacred books. Their work was to contribute much to the conversion of Ethiopia, which continued with ever-increasing rapidity.

CULTURE

The ethnical assimilation of the Semitic immigrants to Ethiopia was rapid and very complete. On the other hand, the newcomers imposed on the local populations their own language and civilization. In spite of the changes wrought by internal evolution and infiltration from without, the Ethiopian language is typically Semitic, and its use penetrated to large sections of the Cushite population. Similarly the culture of ancient Axum is a minority-culture, the more advanced one brought by the immigrants, who also took the lead politically, the Cushites being reduced to subjection and slavery.

At first South Arabian tradition, with a greater or less amount of modification, was predominant in Ethiopia. Later, with the establishment of Christianity, the inspiration derived from the new religion pervaded Ethiopian culture in all its manifestations, and supplied the themes of its literature and of its art. Nothing is known of any pre-Christian literary production, while pre-Christian art was of South Arabian type, and its themes those which the colonizers brought with them to their new home.

On the whole, therefore, though it has certain characteristic features of its own, ancient Ethiopian culture cannot be called original. First it depends on South Arabian models, and later it adopts, along with the Christian faith, Christian cultural elements, principally communicated through Egypt.

Ethiopian literature up to the seventh century consists of translations from the Greek. Outstanding among these is the Ethiopic Bible, of which the first books to be translated were probably the Gospels. Although the Ethiopian church was ecclesiastically dependent upon the Egyptian one, its evangelization, and the translation of which we are speaking, must have been the work of Syrian missionaries. The text-form is not that of the Egyptian recension, but that which originated in Syria and was adopted by the Byzantine church; similarly the new religious vocabulary shows Syriac influence, and although the translation was clearly made from a Greek text, the translators seem to have been deficient in their mastery of that language.

The translation of the Gospels was followed by that of the Psalter, of the Pentateuch, and of the rest of the Bible (excepting the books of Maccabees). An Ethiopian tradition maintains that the Old Testament was brought back by the Queen of Sheba after her visit to Solomon and translated directly from the Hebrew. In fact it is clear from the text of the Ethiopic version that it was made from the Greek Septuagint. It abounds in Greek words and expressions, and has also been extensively revised in later times.

The version is of unequal value. Some books such as Genesis, Leviticus, Joshua and Judges, are comparatively well translated, and the Ethiopic text is here of use in critical and exegetic studies. Other books were less fortunate, and abound in the misunderstandings of the Greek original which are a notable feature of the Ethiopian scriptures, or are abridged, as for example the book of Judith.

Along with the canonical books many apocryphal ones were likewise translated, and several of these have come down to us only in Ethiopic: so the book of Jubilees, or "Little Genesis", the book of Enoch, the Ascension (or Martyrdom) of Isaiah.

Among the non-biblical texts translated from the Greek we may note the *Qerillos*, a body of christological writings drawn partly from the works of Cyril of Alexandria; the *Physiologus*, the celebrated collection of information, largely legendary, on plants and animals, along with moral reflections; and the monastic rules of St. Pachomius, along with an appendix, which seems to be an original Ethiopic creation—at least, no source for it has come to light—describing a vision of the hosts of the good and bad monks. The date of the composition of this appendix is uncertain. It offers an interesting example of a type of religious prose which was to become common in Ethiopia, and we may here quote a part of it:

"Wherefore the Lord in heaven showed me the ways of these wretches, and of those others who are not like them. I saw five hosts of the wicked: the first host was of hyenas, the second of dogs, the third of wolves, the fourth of foxes, and the fifth of rams. Then he showed me the five hosts of the good: the first was of ewes, the second of pigeons, the third of turtle-doves, the fourth of bees and the fifth of she-goats. I said: Explain to me these hosts. He replied: Listen with attentive ear! Those whom thou seest in the likeness of hyenas are the monks that live with their brethren, are coenobites in name, but their ways are like those of hyenas. By day they fast like their professed brethren, but at nightfall, when it is time to go to sleep, instead of the night-watch they go forth in the darkness like hyenas, they go to the convent of the nuns after their greedy lusts, and being sated, carry off the poor ewes of Christ, well knowing that they corrupt women vowed to monastic life as they themselves are; and by them is the ship of their soul entrapped and the wings of their monasticism broken. Woe unto them if they return not to penance! Praise to Christ, who hath given penance for the remission of sins!"[1]

In a similar vein there follows the explanation of the other hosts. This simple and expressive style was to become frequent in Ethiopic, as in other Western Christian literatures.

The remains of ancient Ethiopian art are to be found in the ruins which exist principally in the areas of Axum, Akkele Guzai, and north-eastern Tigrai. At Axum excavations were carried out by the *Deutsche Axum-Expedition* at the beginning of this century; also at Axum, and in north-eastern Tigrai, they have been carried out by the recent mission of the Ethiopian govern-ment. Over the rest of Abyssinia, less fully explored, are to be found other zones of ruins, corresponding to the areas more densely populated in the past.

Civil architecture is distinguished by certain general character-istics. In the first place, buildings were set above ground-level on pediments in the form of steps. Moreover, they must have been very lofty, and dwelling-houses must have had several storeys. From the earliest period, the walls were of the characteristic "monkey-head" type, so-called because of the projecting ends of the supporting beams. This type is reproduced on the large

[1] Cf. A. Dillmann, *Chrestomathia Aethiopica*, Berlin, ed. 2, 1950, p.65.

obelisks, which are one of our best sources for the reconstruction of ancient Axumite architecture, giving us pictures of those buildings of which the ruins, for example, at Enda Mikael, Enda Semon and Tekka Mariam preserve only the pediments, with the remains of the ground-floor pavement and the traces of the walls.

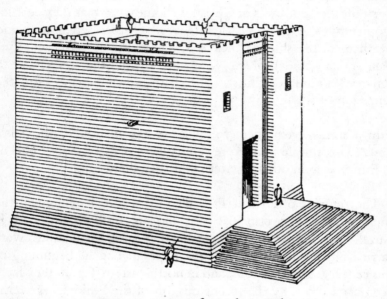

4. Reconstruction of temple at Yeha.

The most ancient of the religious edifices seems to be the pagan temple of Yemenite type at Yeha near Axum. This is rectangular in plan. The side walls are smooth, only the front wall being adorned with a vertical depression, in which is set the gate, led to by an entrance-stairway. There are two windows in the frontage.

As for the Christian churches, the earliest are rectangular in form, and built on the model of the Graeco-Roman basilica. They have an outside forecourt, and their interior is divided by rows of columns or pilasters into three naves. The apse, semi-circular or rectangular in shape, is flanked by two niches or chapels at the corners of the building. The pilasters are square in section, with rounded edges, cut from rock and set on cubical bases; they have square capitals, often in step-form.

At Axum, the chief centre of Abyssinian archaeology, large numbers of the typically Ethiopian obelisks have been found: long slender stone blocks, sometimes left in the rough, sometimes finished and polished, generally rectangular in section, and bearing designs representing many-storeyed buildings.

Another speciality of Axum are the stone thrones, which were consecrated to the deities for them to rest upon, or were used by kings and magistrates in public ceremonies. They are generally made of separate stone slabs forming the various parts of the throne.

Ethiopia is very poor in sculptural remains. Recent discoveries include an interesting statue of a seated personage with a South Arabian inscription. The statue is pocked with holes which are supposed to have served for the incrustation of the garments with gems. Much emphasis, perhaps too much, has been laid on the Mesopotamian influence which seems to be discernible in this statue. The same excavations have brought to light various statuettes of bulls to add to those discovered in the past. Finally there are other items of sculpture, whose purely South Arabian manufacture is confirmed by the South Arabian inscriptions which they bear; these include some remarkably interesting sphinxes.

Relief is represented by incisions in stone, including the well-known lioness of Gobedra. Dr. Franchini has now drawn attention to graffiti on the rocks of the Erythraean mountains: the drawing is stylized, the subjects are for the most part animals of the ox type; there is also a wild goat, which we know to have been a South Arabian subject.

Of painting nothing has been preserved, save some coloured

drawings in caves, representing men and animals. In the excavations at Adulis and other places on the table-land there have been found various specimens of pottery, decorated in a very schematized yet typically local style, whose designs have continued to be reproduced down to our own day.

In conclusion, it is in its buildings that we see the highest degree of development and individuality of this art, in which the Semitic element first imposed itself, only to be in its turn subordinated to more advanced influences from without.

CHAPTER TEN

THE EPILOGUE

THE course of ancient Near Eastern history brought about a separation in culture and ways of life between the various peoples of the Semitic group, whom economic and political forces led into different lands and different situations. To the north of the Arabian desert the Akkadians, penetrating into Mesopotamia, found there populations of different origin and of superior culture, and assimilated the social, literary and artistic forms of that culture. At the other extreme the Ethiopians, soon cut off from the Semitic world, shut themseves up more and more within the African continent, and so became inevitably imbued with its conditions. Nor were the Canaanites, the Hebrews and the Aramaeans exempt from transformation and infiltration. On the contrary, their land, a place of passage and of conquest, reflects, in its continual superposition of people upon people and culture upon culture, the fluctuating course of Near Eastern history. Only the Arabs, in the poverty of their desert, were sufficiently sheltered to be able to maintain through the centuries the same ways of life of their own.

Yet the term "Semitic" does not rest upon an empty abstraction or a merely linguistic definition: the wide variety of situations and developments is traversed by certain constant elements and attitudes.

The fundamental bond of union is language. The strong organic unity of the Semitic dialects would be very hard to explain without reference to the close relationship between the peoples who spoke them.

Another bond of union is geography. The Semitic peoples

lived their historical lives in a contiguity that was not merely an initial one, but one that was reaffirmed and characterized by its constancy.

Nor is this geographical unity a mere external circumstance. On the contrary, it points to a background of common social life, whose existence may well be admitted, apart from any genetic schematization, as a likeness of habitat and conditions within the zone from which historical expansion took place. The Semites, as we have seen, appear in the most ancient sources as nomads of the Arabian desert, who push continually outwards, infiltrating into the surrounding regions and establishing themselves there: from the Akkadians, who are to be seen in Mesopotamia in the third millennium before Christ; through the Amorites, who at the beginning of the following millennium founded a series of states in Palestine, Syria and Mesopotamia, and the Hebrews and the Aramaeans, who a few centuries later came to fill the historical vacuum left by the withdrawal of the "peoples of the sea" in Palestine and Syria; to the Arabs, who much later emerged from their desert in a great movement of conquest which carried them to the remotest regions. These, moreover, are but selected names that stand out in the continual movement, often unobtrusive, often anonymous, which for thousands of years imparted a direction and an impulse to the course of events in the Near East.

The nomads brought with them, as was inevitable, the traces of their primitive conditions. Hence we have sought in the ancient social system of the Arabian desert the approximate outlines of a cultural stage through which the Semitic peoples must have passed, and we have tried to reconstruct, still in approximation, the political and religious forms of that society. These were, in the sequel, the forms which, in more or less evident and more or less accentuated manifestations, we noted from time to time in the political outlook, in the beliefs or the ritual, in the laws, and even in the art of the various peoples. While it is not of itself sufficient to explain their historical and cultural development, the nomad heritage of those peoples remains an element essential to the interpretation of that development, and it is the element to which we have given the name Semitic.

Other bonds of union, though their original unity was less clear, were brought to light by our subsequent inquiry: so many gods with corresponding names or attributes among several Semitic peoples; so many recurring ritual practices. As do the common linguistic features, so too these cultural ones justify us in looking upon these peoples as a certain unity, without denying the divergences brought about in the course of time by changes of habitat and of conditions, and by the influence of the different substrata.

Finally, there are bonds which unite the Semitic peoples not only with one another, but with the other peoples of the ancient Near East. It would be a mistake to neglect these on the grounds that they are not distinctively Semitic. They are for all that still Semitic, and we would do well to see whether perchance they do not include elements which may be regarded as Semitic contributions to the history of civilization.

There is one constant line of thought which traverses the whole of the ancient Near East and determines its attitude to existence, namely, the predominance of religion over all the other factors of life, for which it is the common source of inspiration. This mental attitude corresponds to a particular philosophy of history, one which interprets the world as a single theocentric system.

There can be no doubt but that this conception is shared by the Semitic peoples. It is possible that it is more characteristic of them in their dispersal than in the desert, but this is a question of degrees and nuances, not one of concretely identifiable phenomena.

Semitic history, literature, law and art are thus indebted to religion for their origins, for their content, and for their ends. Historically, we see the rise and the establishment of the idea of universal kingship under the aegis of the god whose people prevails over the others. Literature is full of the gods and their affairs, and man plays in it only a restricted and subordinate part. In law, conceived as divinely revealed, civil and religious legislation is woven together. Art not only owes to religion its inspiration, but depends on religion for its very existence, as is shown by the lack of figurative art in Israel.

So far, the Semitic peoples share in an outlook which is general in their environment; but did they go further than that? Had they their own specific contribution to make? This question finds its answer in the brief synopsis which follows.

Semitic contributions to human culture have been many and positive. In the first place, the very means whereby we express our thought in writing, the alphabet, came into being in a Semitic land, in Canaan. In other ways too the Semitic peoples have influenced the cultural development of the Mediterranean basin: the Akkadians have furnished literary themes, legal conceptions, astronomical data, and mathematical lore; the Aramaeans gave their language, which served as a vehicle for bringing to the West a knowledge of its own culture and that of others; the Arabs through their political organization brought about the conditions for the meeting, in the one great state, of diverse civilizations, and made their contribution to astronomy, mathematics, navigation and other sciences.

The greatest Semitic contribution to human culture is however the religious one. Here the general comparison, of which we have spoken, between Semitic religion and that of the surrounding world no longer holds good. Certainly, Akkadian or Canaanite or Aramaean polytheism bears out the comparison; the Semitic contribution is specifically that of one member of the group: the Hebrews.

The conception, so revolutionary for the rich polytheism of antiquity, of the oneness of God, of a single moral power in place of and above the scattered forces of nature, formed the essential kernel of Hebrew religion, as it was transmitted to the European world by Christianity, and to Asia and Africa by Islam. These three great religions of our world, Judaism, Christianity and Islam, all came into being in a small area of the Semitic region, and were professed and practised by Semitic believers before they set out to conquer the world. When they did set out, their conquest was impressive: the more complex religious structures of peoples in other respects more advanced, such as the Greeks and the Romans, collapsed before the onslaught, unsupported by political pressure, of the religions of the Semitic world.

The triumph of monotheism comes as the conclusion of an important evolution in ancient Near Eastern thought: the godhead is progressively dissociated from the political community, and an independent spiritual community is formed. Christianity, in which this process is carried to completion, forms the bridge between East and West: Semitic in its origin, transcending the Semitic because addressed to the whole of mankind without distinction, it takes firmer and firmer hold in the Mediterranean basin, and thence, resolutely, goes forth to all the world.

BIBLIOGRAPHY[1]

GENERAL

History and cultures of the ancient Near East: H. Schmökel, *Geschichte des alten Vorderasien* (*Handbuch der Orientalistik*, II, 3), Leyden 1957. Chronology: P. van der Meer, *The Chronology of Ancient Western Asia and Egypt*, Leyden 1955. Texts in translation: J. B. Pritchard, *Ancient Near Eastern Texts Relating to the Old Testament*, 2nd ed., Princeton 1955. Monuments: J. B. Pritchard, *The Ancient Near East in Pictures Relating to the Old Testament*, Princeton 1954. Bibliography: *Bibliographie sémitique*, in *Orientalia*, 16 (1947), ff.

I. THE STAGE

Geography of the Semitic area: P. Birot-J. Dresch, *La Méditerranée et le Moyen-Orient*, II, Paris 1956. Historical maps: L. H. Grollenberg, *Atlas of the Bible*, Edinburgh 1956.

II. THE PLAYERS

Languages: C. Brockelmann, *Grundriss der vergleichenden Grammatik der semitischen Sprachen*, 2 vol., Berlin 1908-13; H. Fleisch, *Introduction à l'étude des langues sémitiques*, Paris 1947; G. Rinaldi, *Le lingue semitiche*, Turin 1954 (these books give information on the various languages). Peoples: S. Moscati, *Chi furono i Semiti?*, Rome 1957. Races: H. Field, *Ancient and Modern Man in Southwestern Asia*, Coral Gables 1956.

---

[1] This bibliography is not complete and includes only a selective list for further reading of some essential, general books, most of which are of recent publication.

BIBLIOGRAPHY

III. THE PROLOGUE

Origins: S. Moscati, *op. cit.* Social conditions: R. Montagne, *La civilisation du désert*, Paris 1947; J. Henninger, *Die Familie bei den heutigen Beduinen Arabiens und seiner Randgebiete. Ein Beitrag zur Frage der ursprünglichen Familienform der Semiten*, Leyden 1943. Religious forms: W. Robertson Smith, *Lectures on the Religion of the Semites*, 3rd ed., London 1927; M.—J. Lagrange, *Etudes sur les religions sémitiques*, 3rd ed., Paris 1928.

IV. THE BABYLONIANS AND THE ASSYRIANS

Discoveries. Excavations: A. Parrot, *Archéologie mésopotamienne. Les étapes*, Paris 1946. Writing: G. R. Driver, *Semitic Writing from Pictograph to Alphabet*, rev. ed., London 1954.

History. General: H. Schmökel, *Ur, Assur und Babylon*, Stuttgart 1955; S. A. Pallis, *The Antiquity of Iraq*, Copenhagen 1956. Sumerians: H. Schmökel, *Das Land Sumer*, Stuttgart 1955; S. N. Kramer, *From the Tablets of Sumer*, Indian Hills 1956. Hammurapi: F. M. T. Böhl, *King Hammurabi of Babylon in the Setting of his Time*, Amsterdam 1946. Mari texts: G. Dossin—C.—F. Jean— J. R. Kupper—J. Bottéro, *Archives royales de Mari*, Paris 1941 ff. Hittites: O. R. Gurney, *The Hittites*, Penguin Books, Harmondsworth 1952.

Religion. General: J. Bottéro, *La religion babylonienne*, Paris 1952; S. H. Hooke, *Babylonian and Assyrian Religion*, London 1953. Magic: A. A. van Proosdij, *Babylonian Magic and Sorcery*, Leyden 1952. Divination: G. Contenau, *La divination chez les Assyriens et les Babyloniens*, Paris 1940. Ritual: G. Furlani, *Riti babilonesi e assiri*, Udine 1940.

Literature. General: H. A. Brongers, *De literatuur der Babyloniërs en Assyriërs*, The Hague 1954. Enūma elish: A. Heidel, *The Babylonian Genesis*, 2nd ed., Chicago 1951. Gilgamesh: A. Heidel, *The Gilgamesh Epic and Old Testament Parallels*, 2nd ed., Chicago 1949. Lyric: A. Falkenstein—W. von Soden, *Sumerische und akkadische Hymnen und Gebete*, Zürich-Stuttgart 1953. Wisdom literature: J. J. A. van Dijk, *La sagesse suméro-akkadienne*, Leyden 1953.

Legal and social institutions. Laws: G. R. Driver—J. C. Miles, *The Assyrian Laws*, Oxford 1935; id.—id., *The Babylonian Laws*, 2 vol., Oxford 1952-55. Social life: G. Contenau, *Everyday Life in Babylon and in Assyria*, London 1954. Authority: H. Frankfort, *Kingship and the Gods*, Chicago 1948.

Art. General: H. Frankfort, *The Art and Architecture of the Ancient Orient*, Penguin Books, Harmondsworth 1954. Mari: A. Parrot, *Mari*, Neuchâtel-Paris 1953. Babylon: W. Andrae, *Babylon*, Berlin 1952. Archaeology: A. Parrot, *Archéologie mésopotamienne. Technique et problèmes*, Paris 1953.

V. THE CANAANITES

Sources. Ugarit: C. F.—A. Schaeffer, *Ugaritica I—III*, Paris 1939-56; J. Nougayrol (and others), *Le palais royal d'Ugarit*, 2 vol., Paris 1955. Alphabet: D. Diringer, *The Alphabet*, London 1948.

History. General: S. Moscati, *I predecessori d'Israele*, Rome 1956; A. Jirku, *Die Welt der Bibel. Fünf Jahrtausende in Palästina-Syrien*, Stuttgart 1957. Phoenicians: G. Contenau, *La civilisation phénicienne*, Paris 1949.

Religion. General: R. Dussaud, *Les religions des Hittites et des Hourrites, des Phéniciens et des Syriens*, Paris 1945; R. Largement, *La religion cananéenne*, in M. Brillant—R. Aigrain, *Histoire des religions*, IV, Tournai 1956, pp. 177-99.

Literature. General: G. R. Driver, *Canaanite Myths and Legends*, Edinburgh 1956. Intepretation of the myths: T. H. Gaster, *Thespis*, New York 1950.

Art. General: H. Frankfort, *The Art and Architecture of the Ancient Orient*, cit., pp. 133-201. Phoenician art: R. Dussaud, *L'art phénicien du IIe millénaire*, Paris 1949.

VI. THE HEBREWS

History. General: W. O. E. Oesterley—T. H. Robinson, *A History of Israel*, 2 vol., Oxford 1932; W. F. Albright, *From the Stone Age to Christianity*, 2nd ed., Baltimore 1946; M. Noth, *Geschichte Israels*, 3rd ed., Göttingen 1956. Origins: H. H. Rowley, *From Joseph to Joshua*, London 1950. Monarchy and prophets: A. C. Welch, *Kings and Prophets of Israel*, London 1953. Religion. General: W. O. E. Oesterley—T. H. Robinson, *Hebrew Religion. Its Origin and Development*, London 1930; B. D. Eerdmans, *The Religion of Israel*, Leyden 1947; H. H. Rowley, *The Faith of Israel*, London 1956. Religion and archaeology: W. F. Albright, *Archaeology and the Religion of Israel*, 3rd ed., Baltimore-London 1953. Sacral kingship: A. R. Johnson, *Sacral Kingship in Ancient Israel*, Cardiff 1955. Prophets: T. H. Robinson, *Prophecy and the Prophets in Ancient Israel*, 2nd ed., London 1953; A. Neher, *L'essence du prophétisme*, Paris 1955. Messianism: J. Klausner, *The Messianic Idea in Israel*, New York 1955; S. Mowinckel, *He that Cometh*, Oxford 1956. Cult: T. Chary, *Les prophètes et le culte à partir de l'exile*, Tournai 1955.

Bible. In general: A. Bentzen, *Introduction to the Old Testament*, 2 vol., Copenhagen 1948; R. H. Pfeiffer, *Introduction to the Old Testament*, London 1952; O. Eissfeldt, *Einleitung in das Alte Testament*, 2nd ed., Tübingen 1956. Canon: G. Östborn, *Cult and Canon*, Uppsala 1950. Pentateuch: M. Noth, *Überlieferungsgeschichte des Pentateuch*, Stuttgart 1948; G. Hölscher, *Geschichtsschreibung in Israel*, Lund 1952; I. Lewy, *The Growth of the Pentateuch*, New York 1955. Poetical books: T. H. Robinson, *The Poetry of the Old Testament*, London 1947. Sapiential books: O. S. Rankin, *Israel's Wisdom Literature*, Edinburgh 1936. Dead Sea Scrolls: M. Burrows, *The Dead Sea Scrolls*, New York 1955.

Legal and social institutions: A. Alt, *Die Ursprünge des israelitischen Rechts*, Leipzig 1934; J. Pedersen, *Israel. Its Life and Culture*, 4 vol., London—Copenhagen 1926-47.

Art. General: A. Reifenberg, *Ancient Hebrew Arts*, New York 1950. Archaeology: W. F. Albright, *The Archaeology of Palestine*, Penguin Books, Harmondsworth 1949.

VII. THE ARAMAEANS

History. General: A. Dupont—Sommer, *Les Araméens*, Paris 1949; P. K. Hitti, *History of Syria*, London 1951, pp. 162-75. The Aramaeans in Mesopotamia: R. T. O'Callaghan, *Aram Naharaim*, Rome 1948; A. Malamat, *The Aramaeans in Aram Naharaim and the Rise of their States* (in Hebrew), Jerusalem 1952.

Culture. Religion: R. Dussaud, *La religion des Hittites et des Hourrites, des Phéniciens et des Syriens*, cit. Art: H. T. Bossert, *Altsyrien*, Tübingen 1951; H. Frankfort, *The Art and Architecture of the Ancient Orient*, cit., pp. 164-201.

VIII. THE ARABS

Southern Arabs. Discoveries: W. Phillips, *Qataban and Sheba*, London 1955; P. Lippens, *Expédition en Arabie centrale*, Paris 1956. History: Djawad Ali, *History of the Arabs before Islam* (in Arabic), 2 vol., Baghdad 1951-52. Political institutions: J. Ryckmans, *L'institution monarchique en Arabie méridionale avant l'Islam*, Louvain 1951. Religion: G. Ryckmans, *Les religions arabes préislamiques*, 2nd ed., Louvain 1951; A. Jamme, *La religion sud-arabe préislamique*, in M. Brillant—R. Aigrain, *op. cit.*, pp. 239-307. Art: Mohammed Tawfiq, *Les monuments de Maᶜîn*, Cairo 1951.

Central and Northern Arabs. History: N. Glueck, *The Other Side of the Jordan*, New Haven 1945; W. Caskel, *Das altarabische Königreich Lihjan*, Krefeld 1950; J. Starcky, *Palmyre*, Paris 1952. Religions: G. Ryckmans, *op. cit.* Literature: R. Blachère, *Histoire de la littérature arabe des origines à la fin du XVᶜ siecle de J.—C.*, Paris 1952.

Mohammed and the rise of Islam. Koran: A. J. Arberry, *The*

Koran Interpreted, 2 vol., London 1955. Mohammed: W. Montgomery Watt, *Muhammad at Mecca,* Oxford 1953; id., *Muhammad at Medina,* Oxford 1956. The Arabic conquests: P. K. Hitti, *History of the Arabs,* 4th ed., London 1949; B. Lewis, *The Arabs in History,* London 1950.

IX. THE ETHIOPIANS

History: E. A. W. Budge, *A History of Ethiopia,* I, London 1928; C. Conti Rossini, *Storia d'Etiopia,* I, Milan 1928; J. Doresse, *L'Ethiopie,* Paris 1956.
Religions: C. Conti Rossini, *op. cit.,* pp. 141-65.
Culture. Literature: E. Cerulli, *Storia della letteratura etiopica,* Milan 1956. Arts: E. Littmann (and others), *Deutsche Axum-Expedition.* 4 vol., Berlin 1913; *Annales d'Ethiopie,* I, Paris 1955, pp. 1-58 (recent discoveries).

X. THE EPILOGUE

G. Levi Della Vida, *Les Sémites et leur rôle dans l'histoire religieuse,* Paris 1938.

INDEX

I. SUBJECTS

INDEX

INDEX

INDEX

INDEX

INDEX

INDEX

II. MODERN AUTHORS

III. REFERENCES

1. Biblical

INDEX

2. Akkadian

3. Canaanite

4. Aramaic

5. Arabic